In memory of the Bridal Lane children

John James Bowler aged 4

David Bowler aged 3

Ruth Bowler aged 1

Ellen "Nelly" Bradley aged 1

Preface

On the 2nd of July 1830 the Nottingham Review reported, ".... At Ilkeston also the storm was very severe; windows were broken, and it was with utmost difficulty that the coach to Nottingham was piloted through the sea of waters which ran between that place and Trowell. At Nuttall, Kimberley, Eastwood, and all the way to Alfreton, great mischief was done. At Langley bridge, the carrier's carts waited for hours before they dare attempt to pass, and then it was extremely hazardous. A boat load of coals, containing 40 tons, was lifted out of the canal and left in the tow path, where men had to unload the boat, before they could again remove it to its proper element. Mr Chadburn, miller, of Pinxton, on opening his mill door on Saturday morning, found all the corn floating therein."

This article in the Nottingham Review is reporting on the great storm that hit the region on the 26th of June, the previous week of the report. Over the past 18 months I have researched many news stories concentrating in and around the Ripley and Heanor area and its surrounding towns and villages. Some of the stories unearthed were shocking, tragic and others amusing. The idea to collate and transcribe a collection became an interesting little hobby and I would now like to share the results. All reports have been transcribed word for word including spelling mistakes, as this was a time well before people had the luxury of a spellchecker. Unlike the example given above telling of a great storm in 1830, I decided to choose news reports from the Victorian era as this was a period in which newspapers seem to become more popular as literacy rates grew and the abolishment of newspaper stamp duty in 1855 created cheaper newspapers. A tax which before its abolishment was known as "a tax on knowledge". There is an example of the tax stamp applied to newspapers on the back cover of this book. With the Victorian period came rapid progress in industry, sport, travel and leisure time, thus creating more news.

The first newspaper in the Ripley and Heanor district, according to Mr N Ball's notes on Heanor history reproduced in the Long Eaton Advertiser on

Victorian News Stories

Ripley, Heanor and Surrounding Towns and Villages 1837-1901

Stuart Colebrook

Acknowledgements

Firstly, I would like to thank Kim Durose for his help and advice, and for his design, typesetting and layout in this book. Without his invaluable technical print knowledge I could not have been able to produce this book. Also I would like to thank the Ripley and District Heritage Society, notably Pete Smith for his advice and photo contribution, along with Find My Past, The Florence Nightingale Museum, Picture The Past, The National Archives, The British Newspaper Archives, Elliot at Vintage Frog, Ken for the monument image and not forgetting the ladies at Heanor library for their help finding a photo. Family and friends, who patiently listened to my stories from the past ,unknown to themselves that I was seeking their reaction to each story, which would then help me decide if the story should be included in this book also deserve my appreciation. I would also like to thank Adrian Farmer for his reply to my email seeking advice.

Thank you to anybody who gave me advice however small it may seem. Without all the advice and help given I could not have made this book come true.

Stuart Colebrook

First published in the UK May 2024 by DC Publishing.

ISBN 978-1-3999-8670-0

7th February 1891 was established under the name of The Heanor Standard in 1845. Subsequently it was published at Sutton in Ashfield as the Heanor and Ripley Standard and had a weekly circulation of 2000 copies in a 20 mile radius.

Many people who live and work today amongst the streets mentioned in the news articles collated in this book are unaware of the events that happened all those years ago. Some of the locations have been lost to time and progress, a few of the people mentioned in the stories themselves now have streets named after them. The newspaper reports include murders, attempted murders, celebrations and many newsworthy events. Some quirky stories such as a lion on the loose at Langley Mill, a man prosecuted for speeding at 14 miles an hour in Codnor and an elderly man sentenced to 7 years deportation for stealing a pair of shoes. Also included is Heanor Town football club's marvellous FA Cup run that accumulated in special trains taking supporters to Perry Barr for a clash with Aston Villa. The opening of the Ripley and Heanor railway line was a major highlight within the area at the time. Also included are the convicted murderers Anthony Turner and George Smith, two of the last three men to be publicly executed in Derby, who lived in Belper and Ilkeston. Where possible some extra information was researched and added. I was inquisitive to know what became of the people or what happened after the event. The Jessop Arms Inn, Nottingham Road, Ripley is mentioned on several occasions, and this is believed to be what later became the Midland hotel and in 2023 where a car sales stands.

The book begins with the newspaper report of the coronation of Queen Victoria in 1838 and how this was celebrated in Ripley, the last being her death in 1901. I hope people find the stories both enjoyable and interesting to read and maybe some people will spot the odd ancestor or two.

Sources: The Western Times, Saturday June 23rd 1855
"Tax on knowledge" - see back cover for an example of a 1781 duty paid tax stamp

Contents

QUEEN VICTORIA CORONATION

DERBYSHIRE COURIER SATURDAY JULY 14TH 1838

RIPLEY CORONATION DINNER - Upwards of forty gentlemen sat down to a most sumptuous dinner provided by Mr Staley, of the Thorn Tree and Commercial Inn. The large room was tastefully decorated with evergreens. R Wood Esq, in the chair. On the cloth being withdrawn, the chairman, in a neat and appropriate speech, proposed, "The health of our lovely gracious Queen," Which was drunk by the company with three times three, and one cheer more. "Hail Victoria England's Queen," Was beautifully sung by the Ripley Glee singers. Other loyal and appropriate toasts followed, prefaced by suitable remarks from several gentlemen. "The Queen Dowager and the rest of the royal family"; "The Army and Navy"; song, "Rule Britannia" ; "The Duke of Wellington" ; song "See the conquering Hero comes" ; "The ladies" ; "Here's a health to all good Lasses" ; "The Lord Lieutenant of the County" ; "The Magistrates of the county" ; "The Members for South Derbyshire" ; "The Rev J Wood" ; "W. Jessop Esq" ; "J. Wright Esq" ; "The Rev H Wood and his Lady". The Vice chair was ably sustained by Mr Caparn of Codnor Park. The health of the chairman having been given, the company then began to separate at a late hour, after having done ample justice to the entertainment which was of excellent quality, and conferred much credit on the worthy host. We must not forget to mention that the children to the number of about one hundred and seventy educated in the National School, were amply provided with plum cake, wine, and punch, at the expense of a few gentlemen. Also about 150 females partook of excellent tea, provided for them at the Red Lion Inn. Several ladies presided at the different tea-tables, and general satisfaction pervaded the whole party. Nearly one hundred gallons of ale was distributed on the green. The band playing the whole time rendered the scene altogether lively and animated.

BUTTERLEY IRON WORKS. - The coronation at these works was celebrated with great splendour. A new large and commodious model shop, was tastefully decorated with evergreens and flowers furnished from the Butterley Hall gardens; a number of flags was suspended from different parts of the building , bearing various mottoes , "God save the Queen;" "The Nation's Hope;" surmounted by a crown beautifully executed, the union jack. Over the entrance, was an arch formed with evergreens and flowers &c. Over which was placed a crown of large dimensions, neatly decorated. Four lines of tables were arranged the whole length of the building , (one hundred and twenty feet long) ; at the upper end a cross table was raised, at which the chairman presided. The tables were neatly covered with cloth, and at one o clock, upwards of seven hundred workmen sat down to a good and substantial dinner, consisting of roast beef, Ham &c. Every workman was allowed two quarts of ale. The dinner being over, the chairman, Mr Wm Abbott, proposed the health of our gracious Queen, other toasts followed, the band playing appropriate airs. A number of cannon had been cast for this occasion and were discharged at stated times during the day. On the following day upwards of four hundred females partook of tea , provided for them in this spacious building , which had been neatly redecorated. The Ladies of the neighbourhood presided at different tables, and by their pleasing manners gave general satisfaction. Dancing commenced, and was kept up with spirit until a late hour; the room was brilliantly illuminated, which produced a very pleasing effect. There could not be less at one time, than from twelve to fourteen hundred persons present. The liberality of the Butterley Company on this occasion cannot be too much praised and will be long remembered by their workmen.

REPORTED CAPTURE OF
GOOD THE MURDERER

BRITISH STATESMAN, LONDON SATURDAY APRIL 16TH 1842

Derby was, On Friday, in a state of great excitement, in consequences of this delinquent being brought to the County Gaol there, handcuffed to his captor, who resides in the village of Heanor, eight miles equidistant from Nottingham and Derby. The captor, who keeps a public house at Heanor, was turnkey at Derby gaol, when Good was imprisoned about ten years ago. Good entered his house on Thursday, in the capacity of a beggar. He had a pass, which was pasted on a piece of black linen cloth, and he had attached thereto a list of all towns from Chesterfield to Derby, But nothing about him indicating his previous occupation, or anything leading to a suspicion of his being the murderer, except his dress, which was that of a groom. When examined before – Radford Esq, Magistrate of Smalley, who committed him to Derby Gaol, he was extremely flippant, and professed to be familiar with him as a magistrate on the bench at Chesterfield Sessions. His appearance in every description given of him in the posting bills – his height about 5 feet 6 inches. His captor whose name I did not learn, knew him to be Good the moment he entered his house, and immediately took measures for his apprehension.

ANOTHER ACCOUNT

SUPPOSED CAPTURE OF GOOD AT HEANOR, DERBYSHIRE. – Great excitement was created at Heanor, about 8 miles from Derby, this (Thursday) afternoon, by the capture of an Irishman who was supposed to be the murderer Good. The news speedily reached Derby and other places, and people - especially in this town – were on the tiptoe of anxiety to see the miscreant. On arriving at the gaol we found a large number of people outside, and on entering the reception room the officers of the gaol were in the act of takinghis height, and comparing his person and apparel with the description given in the Hue and cry. Mr Sims at once declared he was not the Good that was tried at the Derbyshire Quarter Sessions in 1833, and who, there can be no doubt, is the person who murdered the unfortunate Jane Jones at Roehampton. He certainly is an Irishman, and is bald at the crown of his head, but in no other respect does he correspond with the murderer, He states that his name is Mccarthy, that his wife is at Rotherham where they have been living for twelve months, that in 1824 he was in the Preventive service on the coast of Kent, and was flogged for being drunk; that he has never been in London since 1827, and that of late years he has maintained himself by hawking cotton. Good or Mccarthy , or whatever his name be, had a temperance medal upon him; he belongs to the teetotallers. He said he is ready to meet any charge of crime brought against him, for that he was never guilty of any. Mr Radford, the magistrate, committed Mccarthy as a rogue and vagabond for 14 days.

FURTHER INFORMATION

Good the real murderer was an Irish man named Daniel Good employed by Mr Shiell as a Coachman. On the evening of April 6th 1842 Police constable William Gardiner arrived at Park Lane, Putney, the premises of Mr Shiell to question Daniel Good and search the property for a pair of stolen trousers Good had allegedly stolen earlier in the day. On searching Daniel Good's work area within the corner of one of the stables, PC Gardiner discovered the mutilated body of a young woman. Immediately Good fled the scene, locking the stable door behind with Gardiner and his colleagues still inside. Within hours a major manhunt was underway. A reward of £100 was offered for information that would lead to the capture of Daniel Good. Many sightings of Good were reported but the Heanor sighting and potential capture was covered by many newspapers nationally. Good continued to evade capture until 17th April while working as a bricklayer's labourer in Tonbridge, Kent under the alias James Conner when a fellow labourer and former Police constable named William Rose recognised James Conner to be that of Daniel Good. Daniel Good was tried and found guilty of the wilful murder of Jane Jones on the 13th May 1842 and executed for his crime at 8am in the morning of 23rd May 1842 witnessed by a huge crowd outside Newgate Prison.

Sources: Morning Post 8th April, Weekly Chronicle 17th April, Lincolnshire Chronicle 22nd April, Liverpool Mercury 13th May, Essex Herald 24th May 1842

The real Daniel Good wanted poster (© National Archives)

SEVEN YEARS DEPORTATION FOR STEALING SHOES

NOTTINGHAM REVIEW FRIDAY AUGUST 8TH 1845

DERBYSHIRE SUMMER ASSIZES, CROWN COURT, WEDNESDAY

Before the honourable Sir William Henry Maule

John Halsworth, aged 53, charged with stealing on the 6th July at Heanor, one pair of shoes, the property of Jeremiah Moore.- Halsworth did not appear to understand the nature of the charge against him, and would not plead for a considerable length of time. On his lordship intimating to him that he believed his simplicity was assumed, and that he would be imprisoned until he pleaded, he pleaded "not guilty". – Prosecutors shoes had been stolen from a room at the Heanor Potteries, and were found on prisoner's feet shortly afterwards. - Guilty. - A previous conviction for felony was proved. - Sentenced to seven years' transportation.

FURTHER INFORMATION

The following transcript is taken from a letter from Mr John Radford a magistrate at Smalley to the then Home Secretary Sir James Graham.

Smalley nr Derby 16 January 1846

Sir,

At the last summer assizes for this county, Mr Justice Maule sentenced John Hallsworth, aged 60, to 7 years transportation chiefly on account of a previous conviction; he was removed on the 21 august + returned on 22nd to Derby,with the certificate of Dr Baily as "not fit to be received into millbank prison, he having extremely imbecile in mind", he is now in the same state altogether as when he committed his last offence + it is not reasonable that so determined a thief should he be turned loose upon the public; under these circumstances I with the commence of any colleagues, invite to ask you to send the governor an order to remove him to the hulks or such other place as you may seem proper.

To the Right Hon *I have the honour to be yours obeyed*

Sir James Graham *John Radford*
Visiting Justice

Smalley nr Derby, 16 Jany 1846

Sir

At the last Summer Assizes for this
County, Mr Justice Maule sentenced John
Hallsworth, aged 60, to 7 years transportation
chiefly on account of a previous conviction;
he was removed on the 21 August &
returned on the 22nd, to Derby, with the
certificate of Dr Baly as "not fit to be
received into Millbank Prison, he being
extremely imbecile in mind"; he is now
in the same state altogether as when he
committed his last offence & it is not
reasonable that so determined a thief
should be turned loose upon the public;
under these circumstances I, with the
concurrence of my colleagues, write to ask
you to send the Governor an order to remove
him to the Hulks or such other place as
you may deem proper —

To the Right Hon
Sir James Graham &c.

I have the honor to be your
Obed Sy John Radford.
Visiting Justice

The letter sent to the Home Secretary Sir James Graham from magistrate John Radford
dated 1846 (© National Archives)

Sources: England and Wales, Crime, Prisons & Punishment, 1770 - 1935

THE TRIAL OF ELIZABETH PARKER AGED 12 FOR MURDER

SHEFFIELD AND ROTHERHAM INDEPENDENT
SATURDAY MARCH 20TH 1847

DERBYSHIRE SPRING ASSIZES, CROWN COURT

ELIZABETH PARKER aged 12, charged with having, at Codnor Park, feloniously murdered Sarah Wardle. MR GALE appeared for the prosecution; MR WILMORE for the defence. The prisoner was a nurse girl to Mr Wardle and was intrusted with the charge of an infant 4 months old. On Friday morning, the 15th of October, she took the child out about eleven o'clock, and was out about an hour. On her return the child was asleep. It continued in that state about half an hour, and when it woke it looked curious in the eyes; and it appeared to be in fits. There was a peculiar smell, and it was thought the child had had ale. Prisoner said she had given it a sup of beer, and afterwards said she had given it a little ale out of a jug in Mr Wysehalls brewhouse. The next morning John Harvey Watson, surgeon, was sent for and found the child in a state on bordering collapse, and convulsed; the child had lost all power of swallowing and had died. It was labouring under the effects of some powerful narcotic. The prisoner said she had given the child some ale at Mr Wysehalls. Mr Wysehall was present, and said there had never been a jug in the brewhouse for the whole of the day. A bottle was found in her pocket. There had been laudanum in it. A girl named Bell, proved that the prisoner had told her that she knew a young woman that was nursing who did not like the baby; that she gave it a penny worth of laudanum, when she put it to bed, and the next morning it was dead. The witness contradicted herself repeatedly as to the time the alleged conversation took place between her and the prisoner, relative to a companion killing a child with laudanum, and as to her own knowledge of what laudanum was....William Henry Fletcher, surgeon, residing at Ripley, made a post mortem examination of the body. In the stomach he found about two teaspoons of fluid – one part milk and the other laudanum. I believed it to be laudanum from its colour and particular smell. The quantity, supposing it to be laudanum, was sufficient to cause death to a child of that age……Mr Wilmore then addressed the jury for the defence, and called witnesses to speak to the kind disposition and character of the prisoner……His Lordship, in summing up the case, said, the only evidence to show that it was a case of murder was that of the girl Bell, whose evidence altogether broke down , from its contradictory nature, and the manner of which she gave it. He directed the Jury, in consequence, entirely to exclude her testimony….The Jury retired; and after an absence of an hour, returned into court with a verdict of Not Guilty. The announcement was received with loud plaudits, which were instantly checked.

POISONER SARAH BARBER AT EASTWOOD

THE SUN (LONDON), SATURDAY JULY 26TH 1851

THE POISONING AT EASTWOOD
Nottingham July 25th CROWN COURT

Sarah Barber, aged 22, dressmaker, and Robert Ingram, aged 19, butcher, were indicted for the wilful murder of Joseph Barber, the husband of the first named prisoner, at Eastwood, on the 24th of March last. The female prisoner is a very tall and rather good looking woman, but on appearance in the dock and during progress of the trial her behaviour was remarkably indifferent and unconcerned. Ingram, on the other hand, preserved throughout an attitude and appearance of the deepest attention. Mr Macauley, QC., and Mr Denison conducted the prosecution; Mr O'Brien defended Sarah Barber and Mr Cockle defended Ingram. It appeared that the deceased, Joseph Barber was a Horse-Jobber in comfortable circumstances, residing at Eastwood in this county. He died on Thursday night the 20th of March, at the age of thirty five years. At the time he had been married to the female prisoner five years; but she had no family. The deceased for some weeks before his death had been unwell, and suffering from pains in the joints, for which he had been attended by Mr Smith, a surgeon, at Eastwood, and his assistant, Mr Mather. Mr Mather left Mr Smith's on the 23rd or 24th of March, or the beginning of

April, and had not appeared since. He was called upon his recognizance as a witness, and upon his non-appearance that recognizance was estreated. It was said he had left the country. On the Sunday before his death the deceased was riding out in a gig with the prisoner Ingram, who lived near him, and who assisted in nursing him during his illness; but he had a bad night on the Tuesday following, and on the Wednesday was so much worse that his mother was sent for. His mother remained with him until 11 o'clock on the Thursday morning, when he appeared better. After she had left he became worse, and at 12 o'clock he died. On the following Monday an inquest was held, which was adjourned from time to time, in order to afford opportunities for an examination of the body. At first Messers Smith and Mather did not succeed in discovering arsenic in the stomach; but its contents were preserved and afterwards subjected to various tests by Professor Taylor and other medical gentlemen of eminence, who ascertained that arsenic was present in sufficient quantities to cause death. The circumstances adduced in evidence for the purpose of bringing home to the prisoners the charge of wilfully administering poison to the deceased were very numerous, and many of them minute. The female prisoner and the deceased had not always lived on very good terms, and on some occasions she had used threatening language towards him. About two years ago she left him for seven months and gone to France with another man, according to the statement of the mother of the deceased; but the deceased went and brought her back. Since that time they continued to live together; and the deceased on his death bed spoke in terms of gratitude for the kindness and attention which his wife and the other prisoner had shown to him during his illness. Both prisoners, however, were proved to have purchased arsenic shortly before the death; they admitted the purchasing of arsenic on the Friday and the Wednesday before; it had been purchased openly for the avowed purpose of destroying mice, with which the house of the deceased was very much infested. The statement of the the prisoners, however, was that the pennyworth bought on the Friday was burnt, and the pennyworth bought on the Wednesday was lost. Neither of them, however, had made any disclosure of the purchase by Ingram of a third pennyworth of arsenic at Bulwell, on the Sunday morning, when the deceased was riding out with him in a gig. The case for the prosecution having been closed, Mr O'Brien addressed the jury for Sarah Barber and Mr Cockle for the prisoner Ingram. The Learned Judge summed up, and the jury found Sarah Barber Guilty, and Acquitted Ingram. The Learned Judge then passed sentence of death on Sarah Barber, without hope of mercy.

LONDON EVENING STANDARD, MONDAY JULY 28TH 1851

THE CONVICT SARAH BARBER. – The execution of this woman, whose condemnation without hope of mercy was pronounced on Friday evening by Mr Baron Parke, at Nottingham, will take place in front of the county gaol in that town on Wednesday morning next, at eight o'clock.

THE SUN LONDON, MONDAY AUGUST 4TH 1851

A petition, which in the course of three days has obtained 5088 signatures, was forwarded on Saturday from Nottingham to the Home office for presentation to her Majesty, praying for a commutation of the sentence of death passed at the last assizes upon the wretched woman Sarah Barber, whose execution is announced to take place Wednesday next.

THE DERBY MERCURY, WEDNESDAY AUGUST 6TH 1851
Nottingham, Monday night.

Preparations are already being made for the approaching execution; strong barricades are being thrown up at various points to break the pressure of the crowd. Sanguine expectations are, however, still entertained by those persons who have interested themselves in order to procure a commutation of the sentence, that their endeavours will be successful. Certain representations have been made to Baron Parke, who, it is believed, has taken more favourable view of the woman's conduct; he believing the statements she had made to the effect, that Ingram mixed the arsenic in the deceased's medicines, and that he did not tell her until after his death.

RESPITE OF SARAH BARBER
Nottingham, Tuesday morning.

The barriers are being taken down, and the crowds of people who have anxiously watched their erection, turn away somewhat disappointed that they are to be deprived of a spectacle. Others rejoice that the woman's life is saved. The extreme exertions that have been used in behalf of the condemned woman, Sarah Barber, have proved successful; this morning's mail train from London, conveying a fourteen days respite. The matter is creating much discussion; some asserting if Mrs Barber escapes, no one ought to be hanged thereafter; others, that she ought not to die, because her husband was such a vile wretch, and others express their gratification because they do not like such spectacles.

THE DERBY MERCURY WEDNESDAY SEPTEMBER 3RD 1851

SARAH BARBER TRANSPORTED FOR LIFE. - The sentence on Sarah Barber has been commuted to transportation for life. She was considerably affected by the intelligence, having deluded herself by the idea that her sentence would eventually be commuted to a limited imprisonment. At six o'clock on Wednesday morning she was taken to London in the custody of Mr Hillyard, for the purpose of being placed in Millbank prison, there to remain until it shall be decided to what part of the penal settlements she shall be sent. The communication had been kept so strictly secret that not a single sightseer witnessed her departure from the gaol, from whence, to the station, she was conveyed in the railway omnibus, her hands being secured by a pair of handcuffs. She has seen none of her friends since she took leave of them before the first respite arrived.

FURTHER INFORMATION

Sarah Barber was transported to Australia on the 4th of October 1851 aboard the convict ship "Anna Maria" along with another 199 female prisoners. The "Anna Maria" arrived in Australia on the 26th January 1852.

That year Sarah married John Hunter on the 23rd August in Hobart, Tasmania, Australia. Robert Ingram was subsequently convicted of felony, and sentenced to a term of penal servitude.

Sources: Convict deportation registers 1787-1870, Tasmania marriages 1803-1899, JF Sutton Annals of Crime.

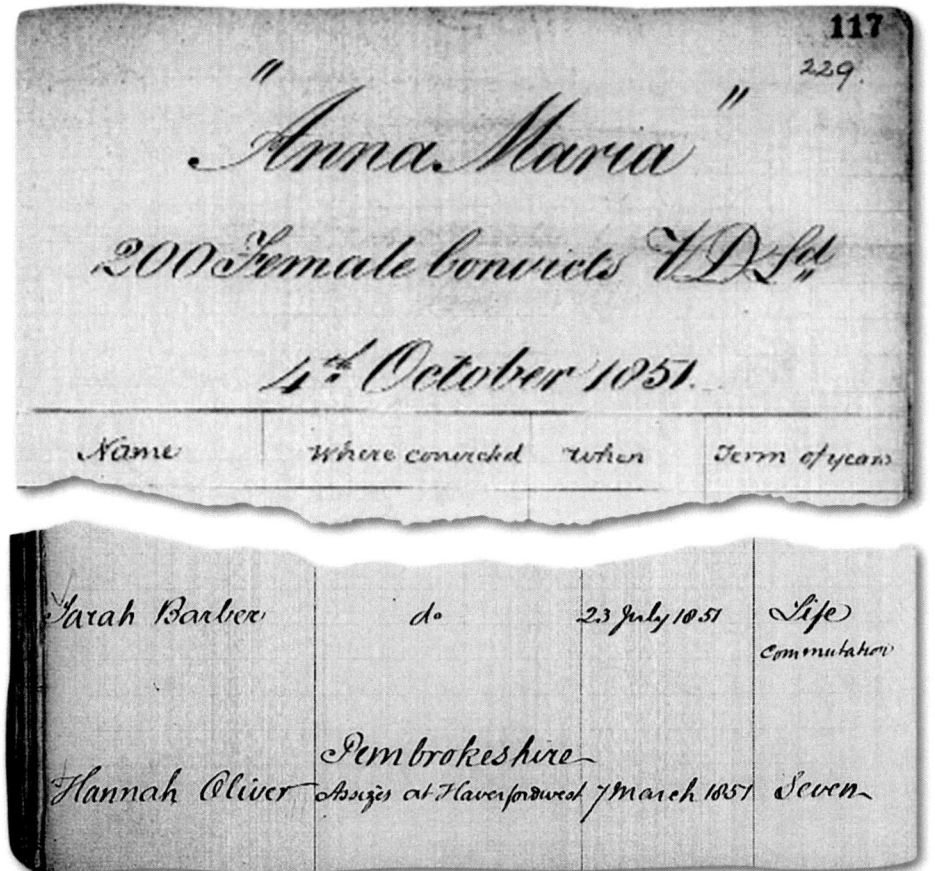

2 pages of the "Anna Maria" convict ship passenger list. The page above shows Sarah Barber's name listed. (© National Archives)

ELOPEMENT OF SARAH BARBER'S SISTER

THE DERBYSHIRE COURIER
SATURDAY SEPTEMBER 6TH 1851

During the past week considerable excitement has been occasioned in Eastwood and the neighbouring district in consequences of another extraordinary occurrence in the family of the convict Sarah Barber. An elder sister of Mrs Barber's, Mary by name, was some years ago married to a collier named Emanuel Wylde, who then resided at Basford, where he kept a beer-house. This man, about two or three years since, however, removed to Eastwood, where he erected an house in Langley Mill Lane, at a short distance from the residence of the unfortunate Joseph Barber, and for this place he also obtained a license for the sale of beer. Wylde and his wife have there resided until the present time, but according to a general report, anything but comfortably. On Tuesday morning, about two o'clock, the husband proceeded to his regular work in one of the Brinsley pits, leaving his wife in charge of the house. He returned at his usual time, but to his astonishment, discovered that she had eloped with a journeyman tailor, taking with her her three children, all the best furniture, and a sum of £145, which Wylde had received a few days before as the purchase money for his house. It appeared that the woman and her paramour had taken their departure in a cab, which had been seen to pass through Langley Mill Gate in the direction of Derby during the day. No information has, however, been obtained as to the whereabouts of the runaways.

SHOCKING MURDER IN DERBYSHIRE

LLOYDS WEEKLY LONDON, SUNDAY JANUARY 4TH 1852

A Most daring and cold blooded murder was perpetrated on Saturday at Belper, about eight miles from Derby, and near the extensive manufactories of Messers Strutt. It appears that a man named Anthony Turner, who resides at Lane end, about half a mile from Belper, has been for some years in the habit of collecting rents for a widow lady named Barnes, who lives with a relative, Rev J Bannister, a clergyman of the church of England, at Field house, Having been a defaulter to a considerable amount, Mrs Barnes sent him a note a few days ago to say that he would not be allowed to collect any more rents, and that he was to consider himself discharged from his situation. On Saturday evening, he went into a provision shop at Belper, kept by Mr Hasland, from whom he borrowed a large carving knife, such as is used for cutting bacon. After he obtained the weapon, he is reported to have said he was going to kill Mrs Barnes with it, for not letting him collect the rents. This was about eight o'clock in the evening, and it appears that he went direct from Mr Hasland's shop to Field house, the deceased residents, and asked to see Mrs Barnes. The servant went upstairs and told Mrs Barnes that Turner wished to speak to her, but she refused to grant him an interview, and the servant returned, with a message to that effect. Turner said he would not go away without seeing her, and, entering the house, pushed the girl aside, and rushed upstairs. The servant, very much alarmed ran to fetch the Rev Mr Bannister, who was in an adjoining building. Mr Bannister immediately ran into the house, and on proceeding up stairs met Turner coming down with a knife in his hand, which was covered with blood. Turner made a desperate attempt to cut the reverend gentleman with the knife, but after a short struggle between them, the murderer was precipitated down stairs. Mr Bannister immediately proceeded into the unfortunate lady's room, where he found her lying upon the ground with her head almost severed from her body. One of the thumbs had been cut off, as if in struggling to prevent the knife from lacerating her throat. Medical aid was immediately in attendance, but life was quite extinct. Turner after passing Mr Bannister on the stairs, as already described, on leaving the house met the servant girl coming in, and he made an attempt to strike her with the knife, but she turned her head and evaded the blow. The murderer then ran off at the top of his speed. He is a married man, has one child, is about forty five years of age, stands about five feet eight inches in height, has very small black eyes, rather forbidding in appearance, and had on at the time of the murder a pair of Arab trowsers and black coat. The most extraordinary part of this awful tragedy is the great ease with which the murderer made his escape, as it was only about half-past eight o'clock in the evening, and numbers of people were stirring about in the neighbourhood. The electric telegraph at the Belper station was immediately set to work, and the news conveyed in a few minutes to Derby, Nottingham, and other midland towns. In Belper, the greatest excitement prevailed, and a crowd of some hundreds soon collected round the deceased ladys house. Mr William Wragg, superintendent constable of Belper, and formerly one of the detective officers of the Derby police, was unable to render any assistance in the finding of the murderer, in consequence of having received severe injuries in attempting to stop the fight some days ago between pugilists Paddock and Paulson. It appears that Turner cohabited with a woman in Derby; and on Sunday, Sergeants Hardy and Fearn proceeded to search the house of the woman, but could find no trace of the murderer having been there. The deceased Mrs Barnes was a widow lady, about sixty years of age, of eccentric habits, and the owner of considerable property in Belper and Derby.

CAPTURE OF THE ASSASSIN

Every attempt was made during Saturday night and Sunday, without success. On Monday evening, however, Turner was taken near his own house. The following are the particulars: - A young man, named George Jackson who lives in Belper-Lane, about a quarter of a mile from Turner's house, met the latter as he was coming in the direction of Wirksworth, about half-past seven in the evening. He felt confident it was Turner, and he walked briskly up to him. Upon seeing him do so, Turner got on the shady side of the road, so as to be out of the reflection of the moon, which was shining very bright at the time, Jackson wished Turner "Good night," as he suspected he was the man. Turner made no reply, but went on as fast as he could; and arriving at the end of the lane, he jumped over a high wall, and ran across the fields. Jackson then hastened to a Public house near at hand, called "Owl Inn," which is kept by a man named Winson, and told the inmates that he had seen Turner. Jackson then hastened to Belper, and called at the lock up; but superintendent Wragg was not at home. He then went to the town office, where he arrived about five past eight. From there he went to Mr Sims, Tiger

Inn, Belper, where he found the five Belper constables, namely, Wragg, Taylor, W Taylor, J Taylor, and Mellor; they were giving some refreshments to the men who had been dragging the river. He told the constables what he had seen, and the pursuit was planned. Wragg and Samuel Taylor went up Belper-Lane, towards Turner's house, and Joseph Taylor, William Taylor, and Mellor went by the shireoaks, which leads to the place where he was last seen. A number of the inhabitants, guessing what the constables were about, joined in the pursuit, and assisted in scouring the woods. When Samuel Taylor and Wragg arrived near to Turner's house on Lane-end, they met a young man named Watson, who told them Turner had taken refuge in his mother's house close by, and they were afraid of harbouring him. The two constables went into the house together, and on seeing them, Turner retreated upstairs, and made an attempt on his life by cutting his throat with a common table knife; but the wound was a very slight one, the constable having struck him a blow on the arm before he had time to do himself much injury. He was immediately secured, and Mr Pym, magistrates' clerk, just then coming up in a light cart, he was put into it, and conveyed to Belper lock up, where he arrived at ten o'clock, an immense mob being there to witness his arrival. The populace yelled and shouted until he reached the interior of the building. Two of the Belper constables remained with him about two hours, and a third one (Mellor) stopped with him all night. He was very talkative. It appears that since the murder was committed, Turner has said he is not sorry for what he did, only he thinks it will be such a shock and disgrace to his wife and adopted child, for him to be publicly executed. He would not have done it if Mrs Barnes had not given him the discharge from collecting her rents on Saturday last. On being conveyed to the lock up on Monday night, he met with a man who has succeeded him as collector of rents; and he is stated to have said to him, "If I had met you, I should have murdered you. I am an honester man than you, though a murderer." We understand he expresses himself pleased that he did not kill Mr Bannister. It has been found out that after he committed the murder, he passed through the lodge gates, crossed the road, and proceeded up what is called "Calvinist Closes," and so got on to the Chesterfield turnpike road. He slept on Saturday evening at the

Peacock Inn, on the Alfreton road, and it is supposed he proceeded, on Sunday morning, towards Mansfield. The landlord of the Peacock Inn had not heard anything of the murder. One place Turner went on Sunday, was a public house where some stockingers were drinking, one of whom who knew him; he drank half a pint of ale and proceeded on as fast as he could. On Sunday evening, he visited a relation near Wirksworth, who having been apprised of the murder, by letter, Turner was not permitted to remain in the house. He was very tired when captured, and had evidently walked a number of miles. He was perfectly calm and collected after his arrest. He made use of several quotations after his arrest, one of which was, "Let the storm of passion be guided by the helm of reason," and he observed that if he had followed out this advice he should not have been in the predicament he was. He says he had words with Mrs Barnes before he murdered her, and that if she had begged his pardon, he should not then have taken away her life. On Sunday he borrowed 5s to assist him on the road. We understand he has said a great deal to the constables, but of course that will not be divulged at present.

FURTHER INFORMATION

Mrs Pheobe Barnes was murdered on the evening of Saturday 27th of December 1851. Mrs Barnes was laid to rest at St Alkmund church, Duffield on New Year's Day 1852. The trial of her murderer Anthony Turner took place at the Derby Assizes on Saturday 13th March. Turner was found guilty of her wilful murder and sentenced to death. His execution took place at 12pm Friday 26th March in front of Derby Gaol, Vernon Street. It is reported that a crowd of approximately 15,000 to 20,000 packed the streets to witness the execution. Never once did Turner deny his guilt.

Sources: Derbyshire deaths and burials, Derbyshire Courier 20th March 1852, Blackburn Standard 31st March 1852.

The above SKETCH of TURNER
WAS TAKEN AS HE STOOD AT THE DOCK.

Sketch of Anthony Turner in the dock.
Derbyshire Courier 20th March 1852
(Copyright © British Newspaper Archives)

FIRST STONE OF THE JESSOP MONUMENT LAID

THE DERBY MERCURY WEDNESDAY 18TH OCTOBER 1854

THE MONUMENT TO THE LATE W. JESSOP ESQ – The first stone of the monument to be erected to the memory of the late W Jessop Esq managing partner of the Butterley Company, was laid on Monday the 9th inst., by F Wright Esq., W Needham Esq., J Radford Esq., Mr Barber, the Rev Gerard Smith, the Rev J Casson, Mr Smith (the oldest servant of the company), Mr College, and the Rev E Davies, assisted at the ceremonial. A long procession of the workmen of the Butterley Company was formed from the different works, headed by the Selston and Codnor Park brass band. A number of flags with suitable inscriptions were carried by the senior

workmen. A beautiful silver trowel, manufactured by Messers Wales and McCullock, London, was subscribed for by the ladies of Ironville and Codnor Park, which was beautifully engraved with the following: - "Presented to F Wright Esq., by the Ladies of Ironville, on the occasion of his laying the first stone of the Jessop Monument, September 1854." A public tea was afterwards provided in the School rooms at Ironville, kindly granted for the occasion by the Butterley Company, at the close of which the party present were addressed by F Wright Esq., and other gentlemen. Throughout the day the village had an appearance of a holiday, all the shops being closed at one pm.

FLORENCE NIGHTINGALE'S RETURN FROM CRIMEA

DERBYSHIRE ADVERTISER AND JOURNAL
FRIDAY AUGUST 15TH 1856

Miss Nightingale – We are happy to be enable to announce that Miss Florence Nightingale has arrived at Lea Hurst, after her arduous and honourable career of public service in the East. Miss Nightingale sedulously avoided that public welcome which would have greeted her had the day or place of her landing in England been made known. She is not less conscious, we trust, of the "honour, love, obedience, troops of friends," which accompany her presence and wait upon her future career. We have the pleasure of adding, on the authority of an intimate friend of Miss Nightingale, that desirous of preserving the strictest incognito, she refused the offer of a passage in a British man-of-war, and embarked on board a French vessel, passing through France at night, and travelled through this country without being recognised to the station nearest to her own residence, where she arrived on Friday last. There, however, on the platform she was met and greeted by Lady Auckland. Miss Nightingale we regret to add, is suffering from the effects of her long and arduous self devotion to the cause for which she has made such unparalleled exertions.

THE DERBYSHIRE TIMES
SATURDAY SEPTEMBER 13TH 1856

TESTIMONIAL TO MISS NIGHTINGALE – The inhabitants of the neighbourhood in which Miss Nightingale resides, desirous of testifying their appreciation of her labours in the Crimea, and their gratification at her return to their locality, have subscribed liberally, and purchased a handsome papier mache writing desk, exquisitely inlaid with pearl, and furnished with choice stationery, &c. On the front of the desk is a silver plate bearing the following inscription: - Presented to Florence Nightingale on her safe arrival at Lea Hurst, from the Crimea, August 8, 1856, as a token of esteem from the inhabitants of Lea, Holloway, and Crich. Miss Nightingale was communicated with on Monday, and expressed the wish that the presentation might be made in as private a manner as possible; and, in accordance with that wish, only a very small deputation will wait upon her and present to her the desk and an address.

Florence Nightingale's writing desk, presented to Florence Nightingale from the people of Crich, Fritchley and Lea in September 1856.
Front cover (left) - Florence ministering injured soldiers
(© Florence Nightingale Museum)

ATTEMPTED MURDER AT CODNOR

NOTTINGHAM JOURNAL, FRIDAY JUNE 5TH 1857

On Saturday 23rd ult .., the village of Codnor was thrown into a state of excitement by a report that a man named John Elliott, a collector of taxes, had attempted to murder his wife. It appears that Elliott after examining the papers relative to the collection of the income tax, expressed himself very strongly that such papers would drive him mad. He had also attempted to get appointed assistant overseer of the poor of the township, as well as relieving officer for the district, thinking these appointments would fill up his spare time. He had appeared in a dull and low state for some time, and several of his actions had caused his friends to believe him to be not quite of sound mind. On the day in question, the deceased, after partaking of a hearty dinner, followed his wife into the house-place and on getting near to her put his hand upon her shoulder, when she perceived an open razor in his hand immediately called for help. A labourer who had been employed in the garden went to her assistance and succeeded, after a struggle, in procuring the razor, which he took away for the purpose of concealing it. During his temporary absence the deceased had taken out of his pocket another razor which commenced to brandish open, and although the wife and the labourer attempted to prevent his committing any act of violence they could not succeed in doing so. The wife received a severe cut which nearly severed her thumb. The deceased then with the razor in his left hand cut his throat in several places, so severely as to cause death in a few hours. Medical aid was immediately obtained but was impossible to save his life. After committing the rash act the unfortunate man said that he meant to have murdered his wife and a young woman who was living with them, also to have killed his cow and pig and then to have destroyed himself, as they would then have all died comfortably. The inquest was held at the New Inn, Codnor, before Mr Whiston, coroner, when the above facts were adduced and the jury returned a verdict of "Temporary derangement."

John Elliott and his wife's resting place. St James Church, Codnor.

(Photograph by the author)

COLLIERY EXPLOSION IN RIPLEY

THE MORNING POST, MONDAY OCTOBER 12TH 1857

The Butterley Company's new colliery at Ripley, Derbyshire has been the scene of a series of explosions, by which about fifteen persons have been more or less injured. On Monday, the 5th instant, an explosion took place, when two men were severely burnt. On the following day (Tuesday), the ground bailiff, Mr John Smith, went down the pit to ascertain the state of the workings, and, while going round for this purpose, the gas ignited and burnt one poor fellow badly, and Mr Smith himself was also burnt, but not seriously. Precautions were taken to prevent further damage from the dangerous element, and, notwithstanding the continued presence of much foul gas, it was considered safe for the men to continue at work while proper caution was taken. Early on Friday morning, however, intelligence was quickly spread that another and more fearful explosion had taken place, by which nine men and two boys had been severely burnt. Their names are George Bunting, Wingfield Park; William Walker, Swanwick-hill-top; Samuel Shooter and his son, a boy, Greenwich; Enos Yates and Samuel Meakin, Greenwich; William Bullock, Ripley; John Green, Mount Pleasant; James Wragg, Codnor; Henry Ivin, Ripley; and John Millership, Hillocks Ripley. Several of the first named are very bad, and serious doubts are entertained of their lives being preserved. Some idea may be formed of the severity of the fire from the fact that a new suit of flannel which one of the sufferers wore was completely burnt to a cinder on his body, and a valuable pony afterwards brought up the pit presented a most frightful appearance, having been literally roasted alive. The sufferers were promptly attended to by Mr W H Fletcher, surgeon, Ripley, who exerted his utmost to alleviate their pain, and, according to the latest accounts, they were doing fully as well as might be expected. The colliery being newly started, we are informed that great difficulty is at present experienced in obtaining proper ventilation until the "headings," now being pushed on, are further advanced and the proper "air-ways" are formed. This is being done with all possible speed, after which the pit will no doubt be worked with perfect safety. The immediate cause of the accident on Friday appears to have arisen from one of the men having placed a naked candle too near the roof. This, we understand, will in future be prevented by every man being compelled to use the Davy lamp.

RIPLEY, Saturday morning

Bullock died this morning.

Mr Coroner Whiston will commence his inquiry on Monday.

THE MORNING POST, WEDNESDAY OCTOBER 14TH 1857
THE COLLIERY EXPLOSION IN DERBYSHIRE

In the Morning Post of Monday, we gave a brief account of some fearful explosions at the new pits belonging to the Butterley Company, Riddings, Derbyshire, resulting in loss of life. Mr Fletcher, the surgeon, has been unremitting in his attention to the poor sufferers. The agents of the company have also been doing their utmost to assuage their sufferings. The following is a list of those already dead, and also the names and present condition of the other sufferers : -

DEAD. - William Walters died at half past ten o'clock on Friday evening, leaving a widow with five children and about to be confined of a sixth: William Bullock, leaving a widow, but no family, died at half past eight o'clock on Saturday morning. INJURED. – Samuel Shooter, sen., slighty; Samuel Shooter, jun. (aged 13), son of above, no hope of recovery; Enos Yates, another boy, very severely burnt, but not without hope; John Green, severely; William Meeking, slightly; James Wragg, Slightly; Henry Ivin, severely; George Bunting, severely; William Millership, slightly. On Monday morning an inquest was held at the Red Lion Inn, Ripley, on the body of William Bullock, aged 29 years, before Mr Whiston and a very respectable jury, the inspector of mines for the district being present. The Coroner, after hearing the evidence, ably summed up, pointing out to the jury where the evidence could not sustain a verdict of manslaughter, because the men had done the best they could according to their judgment, but showing at the same time their utter incapacity for their situations, not only their own lives being jeopardised but also those of their fellow workmen. After a few minutes deliberation the jury returned a verdict of "Accidental Death," with a recommendation that Clark and Cresswell shoud be admonished by the coroner for their future conduct. No doubt steps will be taken by the inspector to bring under the notice of the Butterley Company the incompetence of the baliff Clark for managing a fiery colliery. It may be remarked the the explosion which occurred on Tuesday was caused by Mr Smith, the underviewer to the Butterley Company, and Clark trying for gas with a candle, contrary to the special rules of the colliery.

RIPLEY, Tuesday Night.

Two more of the sufferers, Samuel Shooter, jun., and another whose name we did not learn, died this morning.

FURTHER INFORMATION

It is believed six lives were sadly lost due to the explosions at the Ripley pit;

William Walters 31
William Bullock 29
Samuel Shooter Junior 13
George Gyte 22
Henry Ivin 13
George Bunting 32

Sources:
Derbyshire Advertiser 16th October 1857,
Derbyshire Courier 17th October 1857,
Sheffield Independent 21stNovember 1857,
England Deaths and Burials 1538-1991

The Gleben Miners dictionised by the Butterley Company, May 5th, 1874, without a charge.

| B. Shooter. | G. Brown. | B. Cox. | G. Taylor. | T. Vickers. | J. Statham. |
| J. Seal. | W. Purdy. | T. Wheeldon. | J. Wright. | T. Purdy. |

This image dated May 5th 1874 shows Samuel Shooter (top left) survivor of the colliery explosion and father of Samuel Shooter Jnr. killed in the tragedy.
(Image courtesy of Ripley and District Heritage Trust)

TRAIN CRASH AT RIPLEY STATION

THE DAILY NEWS, FRIDAY DECEMBER 30TH 1859

ALARMING ACCIDENT ON THE MIDLAND RAILWAY - An accident of a serious character occurred on Tuesday evening last, at the Ripley terminus of the Midland Railway. As a train (due at Ripley 7:15) from Derby approached the Ripley station the engine driver appears from some cause to have overlooked the signals, and brought the train up to the station at full speed. As soon as he perceived his error he shut off the steam, but as the rails only extend some 50 yards beyond the station, and before the speed could be materially slackened the engine ran with great violence into the embankment of the terminus, literally ploughing up great blocks of stone several hundred weight each, turning them over with perfect ease for several yards, until it reached the boundary fence next the turnpike road, where it came to a stand. The consternation amongst the passengers may be imagined. By the violence of the concussion they were tossed "pell-mell" in all directions – Men, women, and children in heaps were filled with dismay, and when they scrambled out of the carriages – some rubbing their heads, others limping, and a considerable number using their handkerchiefs to their bruised faces – the scene was exciting in the extreme. Fortunately beyond a profusion of bumps and bruises no further injury was sustained by the passengers. The engine, which was a new one, appears to have sustained considerable injury; the buffers were smashed, and the underwork torn and dislocated. A messenger rode off to Derby to report the accident, and a special train was afterwards despatched from Derby to Ripley. A pilot engine, with crane, was sent up at noon the next day, accompanied by a number of men and several officials of the company. The surgeon to the Midland Company also visited a number of passengers in Ripley, on Wednesday, to ascertain the nature of the injuries, and found all progressing favourably.

Ripley Station pictured in July 1950 long after closure, and for comparison, the site photographed in 2023.
(Authors Collection)

A FATHER MURDERED BY HIS SON

THE STANDARD, SATURDAY MAY 4TH 1861

A most determined and cold blooded murder was perpetrated at a late hour on Wednesday evening last, at Ilkeston near Derby, by a young man named George Smith, aged 20, a twist hand, upon his father, Joseph Smith, aged 40, a shoemaker and a man of property, residing in Bath Street, in that town. On Wednesday the son, George Smith, succeeded in extracting his father's bank book from a drawer in the house, and went to Nottingham with it. The book contained entries of monies paid into the bank amounting to £140. He presented the book at the bank in Nottingham, but the cashier refused to give him the money, and he went direct to a spirit vaults in the same town and pledged the book for a sovereign. He returned on the last train from Nottingham to Ilkeston on Wednesday evening, and proceeded to a public house in the latter town. He then went home, and afterwards returned to the public house, and remarked to one of his companions that "he thought there would be something amiss at his father's house that night." Smith left the public house about a quarter to twelve o'clock on Wednesday evening, and about 20 minutes past twelve o'clock Superintendent Hudson was proceeding along Bath street and met two of his officers close to Smith's house, They heard screams of "Murder!" and on passing under the bedroom window of the house, the younger brothers of the murderer shouted out "George has shot our father!". The police then went into the house, and were horrified at finding Mr Smith sen., lying on his back on the floor quite dead, his brains being scattered about the room and the greater part of his skull blown off. The deceased was in his night skirt, and had evidently come down stairs to reprimand his son for staying out so late and taking the bank book, when the latter deliberately presented a pistol at his father's head and shot out his brains. Mr Norman, surgeon, was speedily in attendance, but death had been instantaneous. As soon as the murderer had perpetrated this horrid tragedy he rushed out of the house in his shirt sleeves and his coat off, to a house of the companion he had been drinking with, a distance of 200 yards from his father's, where he knocked at the door, and said his father had just shot himself. He was at once taken into custody by Superintendent Hudson, who afterwards proceeded to examine the house for the wadding, but it was found to have been all embedded in the brain of the murdered man. They then searched for the gun or pistol, and shortly after daylight on Thursday morning a policeman found a pistol at a distance of 50 yards from Smith's house. It had been thrown over a hedge into a field, and had evidently recently been fired out of. The prisoner was on Thursday taken before Mr Radford, county magistrate, at Smalley, and remanded. The inquest was opened on Thursday at the Queen's head, Ilkeston. As we said before, the murdered man was well to-do in the world, and the murderer was "asked" in Belton Church in Leicestershire, to a girl named Ellen Cox, for the first time on Sunday last. There is not the slightest reason for supposing that the prisoner is insane. He says his father shot himself. The tragedy, as may well be supposed, has caused the greatest excitement in the neighbourhood. On Wednesday morning the murderer wrote a note in lead pencil to his sweetheart at Belton, in which he said he was afraid his father would make away with himself before long. Detective Davis has gone over to Belton to try to get possession of the letter.

FURTHER INFORMATION

George Smith's trial for the murder of his father took place at Derby, on the 29th of July 1861 where George pleaded "not guilty". He was found guilty and sentenced to death, and a date for his execution was set for Friday 16th of August. Three days after his trial and conviction, on the 1st of August George Smith confessed to the crime. He was executed at 12:07 on the 16th of August. The Leicestershire Mercury the following day reported a crowd of 25,000 – 30,000 which was mainly women and children of both sexes attended to witness the execution. George Smith's death sentence was to be the penultimate public execution outside Derby prison as the abolishment of the spectacle came into effect in May 1868. The last public execution in Derby was Richard Thorley for the murder of Eliza Morrow on 11th April 1862.

Sources: Leicestershire Mercury 17th August 1861, Daily Express 17th August 1861, Nottingham Journal 17th August, 1861, Derby Daily Telegraph 22nd December 1910, Derbyshire Advertiser 3rd May 1924.

THE JESSOP MONUMENT STRUCK BY LIGHTNING

THE ILLUSTRATED LONDON NEWS
SATURDAY 27TH JULY 1861

A fearful storm of thunder and lightning visited the locality of Codnor, Derbyshire, on Monday, the 8th instant, injuring the Jessop Monument in an extraordinary manner. The monument was struck near the top by the electrical fluid, which took the zig zag course shown in the Engraving, shattering many of the steps and dashing them, along with the ponderous stones forming the building, a considerable distance, till it came to the base of the building, where it forced the subscription plate from its place, and, cleaving an immense block of stone beneath it, buried itself in the earth. The Jessop Monument is ninety feet high, and, being built upon a lofty eminence, commands a beautiful and extensive view of the Erewash Valley. It is situated nearly in the centre of the Butterley Company's large ironworks and coalfields, of which the late William Jessop, Esq. (to whose memory it was erected), was many years the active managing partner. It was raised by public subscription amongst his friends and admirers and the workmen of the Butterley Company, at a cost of about £700. The first stone was laid by Mr Francis Wright, of Osmanton Manor, on Oct 9, 1854. It was built of gritstone, with a ponderous rustic base, surmounted by a circular column, all in ashlar, smoothly dressed, and firmly knit together by dowels, and a winding staircase worked into the solid stone, thus forming, as it were, the vertebrae of the building.

The Jessop monument in 2024. The modern brick highlights the damaged caused by the lightning strike in 1861.
(Authors Collection)

FOWL STEALING WAINGROVES

THE ILKESTON PIONEER, THURSDAY MARCH 22ND 1866

FOWL STEALING – Thomas Pickering, Collier, Codnor, was charged with stealing two fowls. Thomas Lomas said he kept a beerhouse at Waingroves, in the parish of Pentrich. On Wednesday last, about seven o'clock, he missed a cock and a hen fowl out of his stable; he had seen them both safe there about an hour-an-half before. He saw the prisoner and another man go past his house just after he had seen his fowls the last time; he was confident that the feathers produced, and the bodies of the fowls also produced were those of his missing fowl. – John Barker said he was a police constable stationed at Ripley. On the 15th inst., about nine o'clock in the morning, he went to Lomas's house and there found the prisoner in the kitchen. He said "Pickering, I take you into custody on charge of stealing two fowls from Thomas Lomas," but received no reply. On the way to the lock up, the prisoner said he and James Charlesworth went to see his (the prisoner's father) up in Thomas Lomas's field, adjoining the place where the fowls were, that Charlesworth asked him (the prisoner) for a match, which he gave him , that Charlesworth went into the place and brought out a hen fowl and gave it to him (Pickering) that Charlesworth then went back and fetched the cock fowl, and that he and Charlesworth then started in the direction of Codnor , that on the way Charlesworth said to him (Pickering) "We will pull their necks out," that they went to the Black Horse in Codnor, and sold them for 2s 6d and a quart of ale. Witness had got the fowls with him when he apprehended the prisoner. He had got them from the landlady of the Black horse, and now produced them. – Mary Reavill said she was the wife of Samuel Reavill, and that they kept the Black horse at Codnor. On Wednesday evening last, the 14th March, the prisoner and another man came to their house. Pickering asked her husband if he would buy a couple of fowls; her husband replied he did not want any. Pickering said "there is a little debt standing between you and me, and if you will take the fowls, give us a quart of the best ale, it shall make the debt straight." Her husband said, "Well, will there be anything wrong if I take them?" Pickering replied "In what way." Her husband asked "Have you been doing anything wrong?" Pickering replied "Nothing at all, you have no cause to fear." Consequently her husband bought them for 3s. She had them plucked, and next morning handed them over to P C Barker. She thought it was between a quarter and half past seven o'clock at night when the prisoner and another man came to her house, which was about a quarter of a mile across the fields from Waingroves. – Cross examined by the prisoner: I did not ask you whether they were your father's fowls. You said they were yours. You did not tell me I must get them plucked as quick as I could. I wiped some blood off your trousers. – The case was adjourned for a week.

THE ATTEMPTED POISONING OF A HUSBAND AT HEANOR

THE SHEFFIELD DAILY TELEGRAPH
WEDNESDAY OCTOBER 27TH 1869

Martha Calladine was brought up in custody of acting sergeant Kirkland charged with having on Friday, the 22nd inst, administered poison to her husband, John Calladine, collier, Heanor with intent to murder him. The large justice room was crowded, many being unable to gain admittance. The prisoner, who appeared to be about twenty one years of age, had a harmless appearance. – The first witness called was Mary Calladine, who said she was the wife of George Calladine, a labourer of Heanor, and the prisoner was the wife of her son, John Calladine. The prisoner and her son had been married rather better than two years, and lived at Heanor. They had been living in an house by themselves, and within a distance of two hundred yards from the house where she (witness) and her husband lived, and they had lived comfortably for anything she knew. Her son had been ill and not been at work for the last month. She had gone to see him many times, and he had come to see her repeatedly. She did not give him any medicine last Friday night, when he was in her house. The prisoner bought a powder to her house, and gave it to her husband, who gave it to her (witness), and she mixed it with some treacle and gave it to him. Prisoner said Mr Whitmore, surgeon, had given her a note to go to Mr Simpson's, a druggist, for the powder, before she gave it to her husband. Witness had given her son no other powders. In about five minutes after he had taken the powder he became much worse than usual, and she told prisoner she would go and fetch the doctor. Prisoner went for him, and returned in five minutes, saying he was coming. In about two minutes afterwards witness started to fetch the doctor, who lived about three hundred yards off, herself accompanied by the prisoner. She saw Mr Whitmore who said he would come when he had had his supper. It was about eight o clock when her son took the powder, and it was nearly nine when she saw the doctor, who came in a few minutes. She had seen her son with the same symptoms so far back as five months. One day he went to work, and was seized with a twitching in his arms and legs, and had to be brought home by two men. Charles Whitmore said he was assistant to Mr Boden, surgeon, and had been attending John Calladine for about five weeks. In that time he had seen him as often as two or three times a week. He considered he was suffering from a severe cold, and getting on very well indeed. He had seen nothing of twitchings until last Friday. About eight o clock in the evening of that day the prisoner came to the surgery saying "If you please, I want you to come and see my husband, as he is much worse." He told her he would come in a few minutes. He started to go, and on the way he met the prisoner, who said to him, "Oh, Mr Whitmore, I am so sorry to give you so much trouble. My husband is much better, and has gone down to his own home, so you need not come tonight." Upon that he returned home. In about three quarters of an hour afterwards the last witness, Mary Calladine, came to the surgery, and in consequence of what she said he went to her house directly. He found John Calladine on the sofa, and saw that he was suffering from violent twitchings of the legs and arms, and muscles of the face, several men having to hold him. He said to him in the prisoner's presence "How long have you been taken worse?" The reply was "Only since eight o'clock; only since my wife brought that powder from you." He remarked, "I Have sent you no powder." Prisoner observed, "O, you did not give me a powder, but

you gave me a note to take to Mr Simpson for him to give me the powder."
He rejoined, "I never have." Prisoner then remarked "There were two women
in the surgery at the time, and I am sure you gave me a note." Upon that he
said he would go to Mr Simpson's, and she said she would go too, leaving
before him, but getting out of his sight. He did not find her at Mr Simpson's,
but on returning to Mary Calladine's, found the prisoner there. He said to
her, "Why, Mr Simpson says you never have brought a paper from me for the
powder." She replied that she had taken one, and again repeated that there
were two women in the surgery when he gave it to her. He could not say
whether the prisoner was at the surgery that day before eight o'clock at night
or not, but he had certainly given her no prescription. About three weeks
ago she came into the surgery as he was going out, so he gave her a paper to
take to Mr Simpson's to get a blister to put on her husband's side, but never
gave her a paper for anything else. The symptoms he observed in Calladine
corresponded exactly with those occasioned from poisoning by strychnine.
He went for Mr Woolley, surgeon, about half past nine, and they both
returned to Mr Calladine's house. He remained with Calladine the whole
of the night. There was no absolute danger to his life now, but he was yet
unable to walk from the effects he (witness) should say of strychnine. During
the last fortnight the wife had frequently come to the surgery, and told him
her husband was getting on very well, and that he need not come to see him.
Thomas Starbuck Woolley said he was a surgeon, practising at Heanor,
and visited John Calladine last Friday night about ten o'clock, in company
with Mr Whitmore. He found him suffering from a jerking and twitching
of the arms and legs – that the muscles of his body were very stiff and rigid
– that he was perspiring very much – that he had an anxious expression
of countenance – and that his pulse was very feeble and weak. Such were
the symptoms of poisoning by strychnine and he knew of no other poison
which produced them. The symptoms indicated a large dose. He asked
him for the paper containing the powder, but was told it was burned.
He asked the wife what she had been doing, when she replied "Nothing."
He took her to Mr Simpson's and asked him in her presence, what she

had bought. Mr Simpson produced some packets of vermin destroyer, and said she had purchased one of them. Prisoner denied having done so. Witness then prescribed for the patient, who had previously had an emetic. David Osborne Simpson said he was a registered chemist and druggist, and kept a shop in Heanor. He knew the prisoner, and had seen her husband within the last day or two, but did not know him personally. Prisoner had frequently been to his shop of late, and visited it more or less for the last six years. She came to his shop between seven and eight o'clock last Friday night, and asked for a packet of vermin killer to poison mice, complaining that the last was not sufficiently strong, and stating that theirs was an old house, and that they had many mice. She then asked if he could supply her with some arsenic, as she understood it was stronger. He replied "No, you cannot have arsenic, except in the presence of a witness." She rejoined; "Well, then, I must have the same as before and try again." He supplied her with a penny packet, which she took away with her. He had not sold any of the vermin killer to anyone else that day. He recollected supplying her with a packet about a week previous. The vermin killer was supplied to him by Kiddy and Ashton of Belper, the manufacturer being Mr Adsheads, of Belper. He obtained it in packets as he sold it. The whole packets bearing the word "Poison" Frederick Chapman, druggist, Heanor said the prisoner called at his shop last Friday, and asked for a pennyworth of mice poison. He sold her a two-penny packet of vermin killer, manufactured Mr Greaves of Chesterfield. He believed there was strychnine in it. He asked her if she has any mice, when she replied they were almost worried with them. The further hearing of the case was adjourned till Friday. The prisoner declined to cross examine any of the witnesses, and did not appear at all to be concerned.

THE DUNDEE COURIER, MONDAY MARCH 7TH 1870

On Friday at the Derbyshire assizes Martha Calladine, aged 22, was indicated for maliciously administering strychnine to her husband, John Calladine, with intent to murder him. The husband continued to linger between life and death for several months, and the prisoner was apprehended on the charge of attempting to poison him. Sometime after her committal for trial the husband died, but at the inquest held on the body the jury did not return a verdict that death was the result of poison administered. Consequently the indictment simply remained as an attempt to murder. After the apprehension, the prisoner, after first denying the charge, told Police sergeant Kirkland that she had administered poison to her husband, saying that she did not know what had caused her to do it, unless it was poverty. It was stated in evidence that she was entitled to £6 from a club on the death of her husband. After a lengthened trial the jury returned a verdict of guilty, and she was sentenced to fourteen years penal servitude.

FURTHER INFORMATION

Martha Calladine's original trial was to be held at the Derbyshire winter assizes in 1869 but due to the health of husband John who was too ill to attend the trial was postponed, Mr Huish, who appeared for the prosecution, applied for the trial to be postponed to the spring assizes as the husband was not fit to give evidence. John Calladine's poor health eventually got the better of him and he passed away several weeks before the rescheduled trial on Thursday 27th January 1870 aged just 21. Prisoner 1302 Martha Calladine served her sentence at Woking female prison and after her release she returned to Heanor to live with her parents Edward and Hannah Beresford on Hands Road. Martha died aged 45 in 1892.

Sources Derbyshire Advertiser Dec 24th 1869, Feb 4th 1870, Millbank prison registers female prisoner's volume 3, 1881 Census, Birth Marriage and Deaths parish records

MYSTERIOUS DEATH RIPLEY

DERBYSHIRE ADVERTISER AND JOURNAL
FRIDAY SEPTEMBER 22ND 1871

On Sunday morning the inhabitants of Ripley were startled by the rumour that a horrible murder had been committed in the village during the previous night. On inquiry it appears that the body of a young man, named Alfred Merridew from Newark, had been found in a field on the Greenwich Road. A white pocket handkerchief was tied tightly round the neck of the unfortunate deceased, and on further examination a wound was discovered on the back part of the head, from which a considerable quantity of blood had flowed. Dr Garnham was called, stated that the man had been dead several hours. Deceased had been drinking at several public houses in Ripley on Saturday evening, and about eleven o'clock at night had walked on the road in company with his wife. When near to where the place the body was found, she saw her husband throw some money at the bottom of a hedge, part of which she picked up at the time. The two then parted. The wife rose about half past five on the following morning to look for any remaining money that might have been thrown away, and while doing so observed the deceased lying on his face in the adjoining field. It is said deceased had come to Ripley, in order to induce his wife, who had been staying there, to return with him to Newark. – On Monday afternoon Mr Coroner Whiston held an inquest on the body, at the Jessop Arms Inn, Ripley. The Coroner remarked that, from the communications that had been made to him, from the crowd of people outside the house, and from his own observation, the case was one that would require the serious consideration of the jury. There might be some reason to suppose that there may have been some act of violence committed to cause the death of the deceased. But until he heard the whole of the evidence, it would be impossible for him to give them any information on the subject. And if they had an impression that the deceased had been murdered, or that his death had taken place by some unfair means at the hands of some individual, they would be kind enough to remove such impression from their minds. The case was one that might or might not involve serious consequences to some parties, and required their careful consideration. – Sarah Elizabeth Merridew who had a girlish appearance, said she was the widow of the deceased, who had been a paper hanger and painter at Newark, and to whom she had been married nine months. She last saw him alive at a quarter to eleven on Saturday night, at the Jessop Arms Ripley. There was no one with him or with her. They had been living together at Newark till Thursday, when they quarrelled, and she left him and returned to her parents at Ripley. Deceased followed her on Saturday and called upon her at six o 'clock in the evening, when he was quite drunk. She had no conversation with him, as he was so drunk that he could not talk. When she last saw him on Saturday night he asked her to go with him for a walk, and to live with him again. She declined to do the former, as he looked so wild. And as to the latter, she said she had no objection if he would only keep sober and respectable. He then said that he should make away with himself, and afterwards that he should throw himself down a coal pit. She told him not to do so for her sake. As she felt cold and ill she went home, telling deceased that her parents would feel uneasy unless she did so. He then went away some distance, and threw some money about, She went right away home, and told her mother all that had happened. She then returned to the same place, accompanied by her little sister and brother, to see if she could find the money. Her brother found a six pence and half a crown. They then returned home, which they did not leave again that night. She got up on Sunday morning about half past five, when she and her two brothers went to look for more money. She found two florins on the road. One of her brothers discovered the deceased was in Mr Turton's field. She and her other brother then went into the field, and found that the deceased was lying on his face quite dead, with an handkerchief tied tight round his neck. She unfastened the handkerchief, when blood flowed from the back of his head. She sent for her father and mother, Mr Garnham, surgeon, and Inspector Mosley; they were all soon on the spot, and the body was removed to the Jessop Arms. There were three cows and a horse in the field. After witness's two brothers, Edward and Thomas Hubbard, and her father Edward Hubbard, cordwainer, Ripley, and others, had been examined, Mr Garnham then gave his evidence, which was to the effect that after carefully examining the body of the deceased externally, he made a post mortem examination, and had come to the conclusion that death had been caused by strangulation. He was of opinion that the wound on the head had been caused by a kick from the horse that was in the field, but was quite certain that it had not anything to do with the death of the deceased whatever. After a great deal of consideration, the jury returned a verdict that deceased had died from strangulation, as to which no evidence was to account. The inquiry lasted three to four hours.

FURTHER INFORMATION

Further research revealed that Albert Merredew was the actual name of the deceased and not Alfred Merridew as reported in the Derbyshire Advertiser. Albert married Sarah Elizabeth Hubbard at the Independent chapel, Newark on Christmas Eve 1870. Sarah Elizabeth's mother, father and siblings moved to Ripley from Newark sometime during or between the years 1869 and 1871.

Sources: The Grantham Journal December 31st 1870,   1871
Census, England and Wales marriages 1837 – 2005

GREAT FOOT RACE ON THE TRENT BRIDGE GROUND NOTTINGHAM

ALFRETON JOURNAL, FRIDAY FEBUARY 20TH 1874

On Monday afternoon a foot race, which produced considerable excitement, took place on the above ground, between S Elliott, of Swanwick, and A Randall, of Heanor, the distance being 120 yards, for £100. Both pedestrians are under eighteen years of age, but are regarded as two of the most promising youngsters in the Midland Counties. Each youngster had undergone a special preparation for the event, Elliott having been entrusted to Frank Smith, of Sheffield, and Randall to the veteran Meakin, of Carlton, near Nottingham. The match was made about six weeks ago. Randall it would seem, has won two novice handicaps at Ilkeston, in addition to which he has been successful in a match or two. Elliott ran third to Messers Jamson and Ross's 111 yards handicap on the Trent Bridge ground, Nottingham, at Christmas, and also occupied a similar position in a handicap run at Wednesbury, near Birmingham. Both were in the pink of condition, but as Randall had given immense satisfaction in a private trial, odds of 12 to 8 and 2 to 1 were freely laid on him. There must have been close to 2,000 persons present, and as the men went to the mark the greatest excitement prevailed. Mr T Hind was the pistol firer, and he started the two at the first attempt, the start being a most even one. Randall at once cut out the work, and opposite the new cricket pavilion he was leading by at least a yard, but here the heavy state of the ground began to tell on him, and as it was more adapted to the style of Elliott, the latter gradually passed him, and finally won one of the best struggles ever witnessed by a foot. Mr I Needham acted as referee; Mr Ling of Alfreton, was stakeholder.

CHARGE OF CHILD MURDER AT ILKESTON

THE DERBYSHIRE ADVERTISER AND JOURNAL
FRIDAY APRIL 7TH 1876

Harriett Turner, aged 29, servant, was indicted for wilfully, and of her malice aforethought, on the 12th Dec, 1875, killing and murdering a female infant child, whereof she had been on that day delivered, at Ilkeston. Mr Merewether MP and Mr Sills prosecuted; Mr Lawrence defended the prisoner. – Alronz Spencer, a servant in the employ of Mr Herbert Tatum, of Ilkeston, said that on the 11th Feb he was digging over a mushroom bed in the piggery, when he found an old biscuit tin, which he took to the light, and examined, in company with a man named Mather, and found to contain the dead body of a child. – John Mather, tailor, Ilkeston, corroborated the evidence of the last witness. – Inspector Cowley apprehended the prisoner, who said to him after the post mortem examination – "Truth goes the furthest, and I'll tell the truth. I have had a child." Afterwards she said to Inspector Hancock, in witness's presence, "the child was born in the privy on a Sunday afternoon. I placed it on the seat, fetched a knife, and cut its throat." – By Mr Lawrence: Inspector Hancock cautioned the prisoner, and told her that whatever she said would be taken down and given in evidence against her. Prisoner repeatedly said "Do you think I will get off with paying?" She seemed very indifferent to her position, and behaved strangely throughout. – Alice Cowley, wife of the last witness, and who lives at the lock up at Ilkeston, said the prisoner said to her while in custody "I suppose they have been empting the pig stye, and have found it." Previous to this witness had said nothing about it. Afterwards she said to the witness, "I think I shall get off with very light punishment, as I have seen several cases in the paper where they have done so. A woman at 'Wooden Box' only got six months, and she burned hers." - Mr Herbert Tatum, lace manufacturer, Ilkeston, said prisoner entered his employment on the 2nd Dec and left on the 28th of last Jan. On the first night she came into the house witness thought from her appearance that she was in the "family way." On Sunday, the 12th Dec, prisoner went out with her sweet-heart, and at about four o'clock he saw her pass the dining room window, and he believed she came upon the premises. At teatime however, she was absent and could not be found. – Inspector Hancock, in witness's presence, cautioned the prisoner, after which she admitted cutting the child's throat with a carving knife on a Sunday afternoon, in the privy in the yard, at about half past four o'clock a fortnight before Christmas. Inspector Hancock asked if the child cried, and the prisoner replied in the affirmative. – Caroline Spencer, wife of the witness Alronz Spencer, said she remembered going to wash twice for Mrs Tatum in Dec, whilst the prisoner was there. Prisoner said "They are putting it about that I am in the family way, and I shall write to my father about it." – Inspector Hancock said that on the 12th February he went to the prisoner cell at the Ilkeston lock up, and he had a conversation with her, in the course of which he told her he was going to charge her with killing the child. She said "Yes; I did it, sir." He cautioned her, upon which she said she was determined to tell the truth. Witness said "What did you kill it with?" She replied "with a carving knife," and from the description she gave of it, he went to Mr Tatum's and fetched a carving knife. Prisoner said that was not the knife, upon which he fetched a second knife, which she said was the one she had killed it with. The child, she said, was born in a petty at Mr Tatum's on Sunday afternoon, the 12th Dec. She cut its throat with a carving knife, and it was alive when she did so. – By Mr Lawrence: Witness asked prisoner if she knew that the punishment for murder was hanging. She replied "Yes, but they all don't get hung." – The Learned Judge: Did you put all these questions to the prisoner after you charged her with killing the child? – Witness: Yes, after she admitted that she had done so. – The JUDGE: You must have known that it was very wrong and improper for you to do so. – Mr Robert Wood, surgeon, Ilkeston, said he made a post mortem examination of the body, which was that of a full grown, healthy child. Its throat had been cut, the wound extending from ear to ear, and the wind pipe had been cut through. The child might or might not have breathed before the injury was inflicted. The lung floating test was applied, and they floated in this instance, - Mr Lawrence: The lung floating test was not infallible, and many of the authorities disputed its accuracy. – Mr Hy Geo Brigham, surgeon, Ilkeston, who assisted the last witness to make the post mortem examination, said that in his opinion the child was born alive, its lungs being fresh coloured, and full of air. It was difficult to say whether the throat had been cut before or after death. There was only one appearance which would lead him to believe that the throat was first cut, viz., that the edges of the wound were retracted. – By Mr Lawrence: The child might have breathed, and the lungs been inflated with air before birth. – By Mr Merewether: Crying was inconsistent with the child being born dead. – Mr Lawrence asked the learned Judge whether he thought there was a case to go to the jury, after medical evidence had been given. HIS LORDSHIP said he did not like to take upon himself to say that there was no evidence to go to the jury, but it came very near to the line. – Mr Merewether said he should have withdrawn, if he thought there was no evidence to substantiate the charge which had been preferred against the prisoner, but he could not think so in view of the prisoners own admission that she had cut the child's throat, and the opinion of the doctor that the child was born alive. – Mr Lawrence addressed the jury on behalf of the prisoner, and contended that there was no evidence to show that the child was born alive. Mr Brigham's opinion, no doubt, inclined to that supposition, but he asked the jury if they could find the prisoner guilty of the most serious offence known to law, merely because of the impression left upon the mind of a scientific man? – The Learned JUDGE, in summing up, said the jury, before they could find the prisoner guilty of this charge, must not only be satisfied that the child was born alive, but that it was killed by the wound which the prisoner admitted she had inflicted upon its body. – The jury retired, and upon their return into court stated, through their foreman, that they found her guilty of concealment of birth, and the judge remarked that it was a very serious case, sentenced the prisoner to 18 months' imprisonment, with hard labour.

GREAT FIRE AT LANGLEY MILL DISGRACEFUL SCENES

THE SHEFFIELD DAILY TELEGRAPH
MONDAY JULY 3RD 1876

LANGLEY MILL, SUNDAY.-About seven o'clock this morning (Sunday) a fire broke out on the extensive premises of Messrs, Smith and Bowes' flour mills, Langley Mill. Langley Mill is 9 ½ miles from Nottingham, and five from Ripley. The fire originated in the new wing of the above building. Messengers were at once despatched to Ripley for the engine belonging to J.Crossley. Esq., at the factory, and also the fire engine belonging to the Butterley Company. A small engine was also sent for from Shipley: a telegram for aid was also sent to Nottingham. Being Sunday morning thousands of people were soon on the spot. The first engine to arrive was that from Mr Crossley's, Ripley, and this was speedily followed by the one from Shipley. As the Cromford canal runs near to the above steam flour mills, a plentiful supply of water was soon obtained. Before the arrival of the engines, the entire roof of the building fell in with a tremendous crash. The efforts of the Shipley engine were directed to save the north end of the building, and those of the Ripley engine were confined to the south end. The fire was raging furiously when the Nottingham engine arrived, which was quickly followed by the Butterley Company's engine. All the engines were soon set to work, but the fire had soon got to the mastery, and at eight o'clock the large building was completely gutted. The other wing of the building was full of bags of flour, and hundreds of willing hands assisted in removing them by means of waggons and railway trucks, carrying them to a place of safety. The crowd at one time would number at least ten thousand people. The proprietor of the mills, Mr W Smith, is one of the leading Wesleyans of the district. The firm of which he is a prominent member some years ago built and presented a beautiful Wesleyan Chapel to the society at Langley Mill. The Sunday school sermons were announced to the preached at the above place today (Sunday), by Mr Harrison, of Derby, late of Ripley, but in consequence of the fire the services had to be postponed. The greatest excitement prevailed during the forenoon, and numerous visitors came from Nottingham, Ilkeston, Ripley, Eastwood, and other places. Superintendent Hancock and a large body of police were in attendance, but the crowd was so large and disorderly that their efforts were almost futile in such a scene of confusion. It became absolutely necessary to throw water on the crowd before they would disperse. News of the fire was at once conveyed to Mr J Copestake of Ripley, brother in law to the widow of the late Mr Bowes and one of his executors. The mill has been in active operation for some years past, and supplied shopkeepers at Ripley and surrounding places. The old part of the mill, which was not connected with the scene of the present disaster, was discovered to be on fire, but soon extinguished. Books, papers, and other business documents were at once removed from the office. The fire was burning furiously at 11.30. At two o'clock Mr Crossley's engine arrived in Ripley. The firemen reported that to a great extent the fire had been got under. The origin of the conflagration is not known at present. The loss will be several thousands, and many hands thrown out of employment. It is believe the building is insured.

STRIKE OF NAILERS

THE NOTTINGHAM JOURNAL, SATURDAY JUNE 16TH 1877

BELPER – The Belper nailers having received from the Staffordshire nailers a letter intimating that they had struck work in consequence of the notice of a reduction of three pence per thousand, issued by their employers a fortnight ago having expired, a meeting was held at the Denby arms to consider what was to be done in the event of the Belper masters, as is generally the case, following the example of the Staffordshire employers and giving a fortnights notice of an equal reduction. It seemed to be the opinion of the meeting that if a notice of reduction was given it should be resisted, and that a strike would be unavoidable, as a reduction had been submitted to only about two months back. A deputation was at length appointed by the meeting to wait on the Belper nail manufacturers and ascertain what, under the circumstances, they intended doing, and the meeting then adjourned.

THE DERBYSHIRE COURIER SATURDAY JUNE 23RD 1877

A portion of the Belper nailers are out on strike, in consequence of 3d per 1000 nails having been deducted, without notice from their wages. They have refused to take out anymore iron until the 3d is returned, and unless they are paid the old price. Those who are not out on strike are supporting them. The strike in Staffordshire still continues, and is not likely to come to an end.

FATAL FIRE IN BRIDLE LANE

THE MANCHESTER EVENING NEWS
WEDNESDAY JANUARY 21ST 1880

Last night a fire broke out in Bridle Lane, Ripley, Derbyshire, in a dwelling house occupied by James Bowler. The fire was first discovered by some passers by, who raised the alarm. A Ladder was procured, and a plentiful supply of water being available, efforts were at once made to arrest the progress of the flames. An exploration was made of the premises, when four children were found in one bed. They were lowered from the window to the street, but upon examination it was found that all of them were dead, having been apparently suffocated in their sleep. Both Bowler and his wife were out at the time of the occurrence. The floor of the bedroom was very much charred, and some of the furniture in the lower rooms was burnt, but the cause of the fire is unknown. The remains of the children were removed prior to the inquest being held.

Bridle Lane in 2023
(Authors Collection)

THE DERBY DAILY TELEGRAPH AND REPORTER
SATURDAY JANUARY 23RD 1880

THE FATAL FIRE AT RIPLEY
THE INQUEST ON THE BODIES

Mr W H Whiston held an inquest at the Jessop arms, Ripley, on Thursday on the bodies of James John Bowler, David Bowler, Ruth Bowler and Ellen Bradley, the four children who were suffocated on Tuesday at Ripley. Evidence was adduced as follows :- Mr Marshal Hooper: I am a surgeon practising in Ripley. On Tuesday night the 20th January, I was sent for to a house in Bridle lane, Greenwich, Ripley, occupied by James Bowler. On arriving there I found three children in a neighbour's house, two boys and a girl. They were all dead, having died from suffocation. They were all blackened on one side of the face, and there were also marks of burning on them, especially on the girl, apparently blackened by smoke and scorching. I went to another house and found the fourth child. She was dead, and was black in the face. The children could not have been dead more than 15 or 20 minutes when I saw them. I do not think the children could have been a minute in the suffocating atmosphere before they died. I do not think, from the appearance of the bodies, that any of them were awake except the little one. – Elizabeth Bowler: I am the wife of James Bowler and I live in Bridle lane, Ripley, My husband is a miner. Three of the bodies seen are those of our children, John James Bowler, aged four years last May, David Bowler aged three years last August, and Ruth Bowler, aged one last July. The body of the other child is that of Ellen Bradley. She was the illegitimate child of Ellen Bradley, of Nottingham. The child was at nurse at my house. I was at home on Tuesday night with the four children in the house. My husband was at home all day, and left the house at seven o'clock in the evening. All four children were undressed ready for bed when he went out. After he went out they were put to bed. They all lay in one bed in the room over the kitchen, the bed being on the nearest the side of the house to the lane. David lay nearest the stairs, John James was next, Ruth next, and then Nelly.

After I had put the children to bed I mended the fire, and put some slack on, and washed and dressed myself. I afterwards went to look at the children and found them all fast asleep. I then went out of the house, leaving the children alone by themselves in the house. I have occasionally left them before, when both I and my husband have been obliged to go out. There was a clear fire burning. There was a high guard round the fire when I left, but there were no clothes on it. There was a piece of cocoa matting on the floor, but it was some distance from the range. There was a wooden mantle shelf about the fire place, but nothing on it was likely to catch fire. There was a sofa under the window covered in print. There was a wooden cradle in the corner with a chaff mattress in it. The children's clothes were in the cradle. The gas meter stood in the corner of the room by the side of the fireplace. I drew all things away from the fireplace before I left. There were two tables in the room. As I was coming home I saw a policeman and heard something said about Bridle lane. I thought there was something amiss. When I got to the gate of my house I met my father and husband, and they took me away. I did not know what had happened for some time. I have not perceived any leakage of gas in the house since three months ago, when my husband stopped it. The chimney was swept a month or six weeks ago. – William Kemp, a joiner, deposed that on Tuesday night he heard there was a fire in Bridle lane. He went to Bowlers house, and on entering found it full of smoke. The flames had been extinguished. He made his way upstairs and took the children out of bed. He handed them into the street through the window. The fire had burned most of the furniture of the room and the floor above. The greatest damage was done to the part of the room opposite the fireplace. He believed the lead piping hung from the ceiling. – Samuel Hemmingway, a miner, said he was informed on Tuesday night that there was a fire. He went to Bowler's, and found that it was in flames. A ladder was put to the bedroom window, and the children were with great difficulty got out of the room. "Hard coal tops" would fly out of the fire sometimes more than soft slack, and might possibly set cocoa matting on fire. There was a great deal of sulphur in that coal. – George White, a planner at the Butterley Ironworks, and living next door to the bowlers, gave evidence which was merely a corroboration of that of the previous witnesses. – Inspector Cook spoke to going to the fire on Tuesday night. The children had just been taken out of the room, and the fire was then put out. The room was badly damaged. – The jury returned a verdict of "Accidentally suffocated," and added that they highly deprecated the practice of leaving children alone in a house without some person in proper charge of them.

A POLICEMAN SHOT NEAR RIPLEY

THE DERBY DAILY TELEGRAPH
TUESDAY OCTOBER 3RD 1882

On Monday, an event took place at Marehay, near Ripley, which caused great excitement. A man named James Harrison, alias Atlow, a miner, 45 years of age, was in the Miner's arms Marehay, when he quarrelled with another man named Stone, who resides near Harrison at Marehay. Harrison had a gun in his possession and threatened to shoot Stone, who, fearing that he would carry his threat into execution, sent for a policeman. Upon the arrival of police constable Swift, Harrison and Stone both left the public house, accompanied by Swift. The officer told Harrison to take his gun home, but he said he would not, and immediately he discharged it at the police officer, and the contents entered his arm, hand, and face, injuring him severely. The unfortunate man was conveyed to his lodgings and medical aid obtained. His injuries are said to be of a very serious character. Information was at once given to Inspector Cook, at Ripley, and in company with Police constables Keeling and Fearn, they proceeded to the residence of Harrison, where they apprehended him and took him to Ripley lock up. The police found three guns in his house, which they took possession of, and conveyed to Ripley.

ATTEMPTED MURDER OF A POLICEMAN

THE LEICESTER DAILY MERCURY
SATURDAY NOVEMBER 4TH 1882

THE TRIAL – Leicester Assizes

JAMES HANSON HARRISON 42, collier, was charged with feloniously and maliciously shooting at one John Swift with a gun loaded with powder and shot, with intent to murder. – The prosecution having been opened by Mr Mozley, the prosecutor, John Swift, a policeman stationed at Derby, was called. He stated that on the 2nd October last he was called into the Miner's Arms Marehay, near Ripley, about half past eleven o'clock in the forenoon. Inside the house he found the prisoner, who had a gun in his possession. He subsequently saw the prisoner outside the house holding his gun in his hands as if intending to shoot something in the air. Witness remonstrated with him, and said that he would shoot someone if he was not careful, and told him to take the gun home before there was an accident. Prisoner said "don't you interfere, or you will know about it," and after some more words he placed the gun almost to his shoulder and placed the muzzle against the breast of the witness. He then saw him placing his finger on the trigger, and immediately he seized the barrel, and held it above his head. The prisoner tried to get possession of the gun, and took two swinging kicks at the witness, rendering the latter almost unconscious, and obliging him to leave hold of the prisoner, at the same time pushing the prisoner inside the public house and shutting the door. He held the door for some time and becoming weak from the injuries he had received, endeavoured to run into a house up the road, but the moment he released hold of the door, the prisoner sprang out and shot at him, striking him on the head and hand. Witness then fell down insensible, and was removed into a house. William Stone, miner, Marehay, said that on the day in question he had a quarrel with the prisoner at the Miners Arms and the prisoner followed him outside the house and fired both barrels up in the air near witness, saying afterwards he would knock his brains out with the butt end. He thereupon sent for the constable. – Dr Allen, of Ripley, stated that he examined the prosecutor and found him suffering from wounds to the head and hand. – This concluded the evidence for the prosecution, and Mr Weightman addressed the jury for the defence.

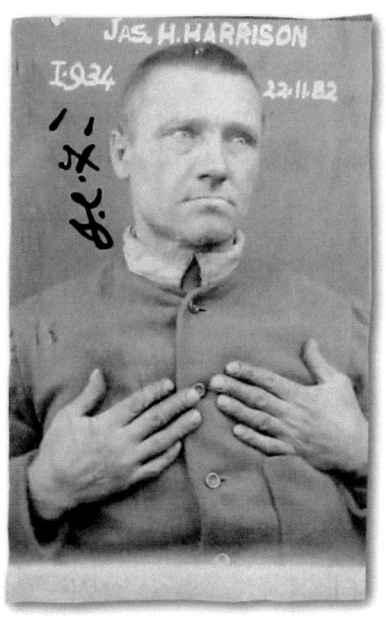

James Hanson Harrison
(© National Archives)

He said the question was whether when the prisoner fired the gun he intended to murder, and examined the evidence for the prosecution to show that such was not the case. If the jury were of the opinion that the prisoner did not fire with murderous intent then the case reduced itself to one of malicious wounding, and for this the prisoner had rendered himself liable to a penalty, but not one so serious as it would have been were he found guilty on the more grave count. – The jury did not find the prisoner guilty of the count of charging him with the intent to murder, but guilty of maliciously wounding with intent to do grievous bodily harm. – Sentence deferred.

FURTHER INFORMATION

James Hanson Harrison was found guilty of maliciously wounding Police Constable John Swift with intent to do grievous harm and sentenced to 5 years penal service. He served his sentence at Leicester, Pentonville and Portsmouth prisons before being released on license in October 1886.

Sources: England & Wales, Crime, Prisons & Punishment, 1770 – 1935. Home Office and Prison Commission: Male licenses

FURIOUS DRIVING AT CODNOR

THE LONG EATON ADVERTISER
SATURDAY OCTOBER 28TH 1882

FURIOUS DRIVING. – William Bell was charged with furious driving at Codnor on September 27th. – Inspector Cook, of Ripley said that the day named he was going to Langley Mill, and was driving about 10 miles an hour. On the way he met defendant with a brewery waggon which he was driving at the rate of 14 miles an hour. He was passing through Codnor at the time, and appeared to be under the influence of drink. – Defendant pleaded guilty, and was fined £1 and costs.

DOUBLE MURDER ATTEMPT NEAR RIPLEY

THE LONG EATON ADVERTISER
SATURDAY JUNE 16TH 1883

The serpent was in Eden. The fairest, loveliest spots on earth are sometimes the scenes of the most diabolical crimes. No one who knows Greenwich, close to Ripley, and enjoyed its tranquil beauty, would expect that one day it should be talked of as a place in which a dreadful and dastardly tragedy had been enacted. Yet, there is now in prison, awaiting the trial that he will have to face, a man who has desecrated the innocence of Greenwich as Satan destroyed the happiness of Paradise. A respectable woman and her daughter were living in Greenwich. They bore a good reputation. Unfortunately for their peace, the daughter Alice Seal, about 24 years of age, a while back married one Thomas Spick, a journeyman brewer. The fellow proved to be a drunken, dissipated, and brutal creature, and ill-used his wife to such degree that she insisted on separation, but not before she had to appeal to the law, and get him bound over. His character was too bad to justify anybody in being surety for his behaviour, and, in default, he was committed to Nottingham jail. It is supposed he was released on Tuesday, for on that day he returned to Greenwich, and went to the house where his wife was residing with her mother. What his intention was in troubling them with his presence is not quite plain. Apparently, he wished to renew cohabitation, for he pleaded with her to "give" him "another chance." Whether he meant to try and treat her better if she had yielded, cannot be ascertained. Even if such a resolve had been formed by him, the probability is that he would very soon have broken it. His wife no doubt was convinced of this, and refused to have any further communication with him. After abusing her and her mother with foul and violent language, the enraged scoundrel pulled a revolver from his pocket and deliberately shot them both in the head. There was no witness of the attempted murder, and the actual incidents attending it can only be surmised. Spick having thus accomplished his purpose, whether the execution of it was dependent or not on the reception which he met with, retired to a neighbouring public house, leaving his victims insensible and all but dead. His conduct at the public house aroused suspicions, the police were informed of these suspicions and Spick was arrested, while surgical aid was rendered to Mrs Seal and he daughter. At first the cases seemed to be desperate and no hope was entertained of the recovery of either woman. The younger one, being in a condition that would have move the sympathy of almost any other husband, was considered to be in more imminent danger, as the medical men were afraid to do anything to find and extract the bullet. The latest accounts, however, are better, and it is thought both the mother and her daughter have a chance of life. As for the wretch who has blighted their existence, his doom is certain and richly deserved. He will have either to end his days on the gallows, or drag them out in penal servitude.

DERBYSHIRE ADVERTISER AND JOURNAL
FRIDAY AUGUST 3RD 1883

CROWN COURT, Monday
[Before Mr Justice Smith]
THE RIPLEY SHOOTING CASE

Thomas Robert Spick, aged 28, brewer, was indicated for feloniously wounding Ann Spick and Sarah Seal, with intent to kill and murder them, at Pentrich, on June 12th. Mr Tonman Mosley prosecuted; prisoner being defended by Mr Wightman.

Mr Mosley, in opening the case, said the prisoner's wife whom he was charged with shooting, was the daughter of Mary Seal, who lived at Greenwich, Ripley. In consequence of some disagreement between prisoner and his wife, caused him to be bound over to keep the peace towards her and then went to live with her mother at Ripley. When his wife left him he went to lodge with Thomas Glover, at Nottingham, and before the 11th of June he was alleged to have used expressions to the effect that if his wife would not return and live with him he should put a bit of lead into her and her mother. Glover did not take much notice of these expressions, believing he was only joking. On the 8th of June he went to a shop in Nottingham, where he brought a six-chambered revolver and cartridges. On the evening of the 11th June he went a walk with Arthur Holmes, and while they were together he said he was going to New York on the following day. On that occasion he fired the revolver at a gatepost, and Holmes aimed several shots at the post also. Later at night he went the house of a man named Taylor, where he slept. He left there about eight o'clock the next morning, saying he should return at night, but that if anybody enquired for him they were to be told that he had left. He appeared to have gone straight from Nottingham to the house of his mother-in-law at Ripley, arriving about half past eleven. He was not allowed to enter the house, and remained outside talking to his wife and her mother. He asked her to go and live with him again, and she refused; but there was no altercation – simply a request and a refusal. Between half past eleven and one o'clock he went to the house of a Mrs Butler, who lived next door and asked for a drink of water, which was given to him. He seemed so strange and excited that she was frightened by his appearance, and she locked the door after he had gone away. Directly after he had gone out he went again to his mother-in-law's door. He commenced talking to her and his wife, something being said about prisoner having borrowed money from a Mrs Fletcher, who was at the time staying at Ripley. Mrs Fletcher was sent for and asked about the borrowed money. While she was there again the prisoner again requested his wife to go and live with him. She replied, "No, Tom, I would sooner go to the workhouse than come back again, as I should be in fear of my life." He was seen by Mary Seal to put his hand in his pocket and pull out a revolver, which he fired. Mrs Spick was struck, and she fell to the floor. He then fired another shot at her mother, who was also wounded and fell. Four doctors were sent for, and one of them, Mr Allen, would be called. He would state that he found a bullet wound behind Mrs Spick's ear, and two wounds - one on the cheek and the other behind the ear – on Mrs Seal. Both women were dangerously ill for some days, and their depositions were taken. After this occurrence he moved away, pointing the revolver as he did so at Mrs Fletcher. He then tried the door of Mrs Butler, to which he crawled on his hands and knees, but he was unable to open it, and then went down the road. On the way he was seen by Charles Smith, who spoke to him and followed him into the Jessop's Arms, which was kept by Mrs Clarke. He went straight into the bar, where there were some men either eating or drinking, and he seized a carving knife which he was putting towards his throat, when it was taken from him. He afterwards began to do something with a revolver, but it was taken from him, as well as some cartridges by a man named Needham. When given into the custody of police constable Wagstaff he said he did not know what he was doing, and enquired the charge. Later on he asked repeatedly whether the women were dead, and said that if they got better he should think he should not get above 20 years. The following evidence was then given: - Ann Spick said she was the wife of the prisoner, and was living with at Nottingham until the 3rd of February. She had been married to him seven years last April, and had two children. On the 3rd of February she took him before the magistrates at Nottingham, and caused him to be bound over to keep the peace. That evening she went to a neighbour's house to stay out of her husband's way. She telegraphed the same night to her mother, who came out to see her. She afterwards went to live with her mother at Greenwich, Ripley, until the 12th of June. She only saw her husband once in the meantime. On the 12th of June witness's husband went to her mother's house. She was not expecting him. He went to the back door, but her mother told him she would not allow him to enter. He replied "alright, mother I'll stand here" Witness then went to the door, and he asked her if she would live with him again. She declined several times, but at his request shook hands with him. He remained near the house until nearly one o'clock, and while he was there witness and her mother had their dinner. During a conversation which ensued witness and her mother referred to his having borrowed money from Mrs Fletcher. He denied that he had done so, in consequence of which Mrs Fletcher was sent for, After that prisoner again asked witness to live with her, but she said "No, Tom, I would rather go to the workhouse than live with you, as I am in fear of my life." At that time she was near her mother's doorstep, and while her attention was directed to something in the house she heard the report of a firearm and was shot at the back of the right ear. She fell to the floor, and heard a second shot fired. She was faint for a time, and on recovering consciousness saw her mother, who was bleeding from two wounds, leaning over a water tub. Witness was put on chairs in the yard, and remained in bed about a fortnight. Cross-examined – She lived happily with her husband during the first part of her married life. He was always addicted to drink. He was under the influence of drink when he ill-treated her before being bound over to keep the peace. She was not aware that he had a stroke on the right side, but something came to his face that which drew it aside. A little drink did not have a more serious effect upon him than previously. She had a child before her marriage by a man named Fletcher, who then lived at Ripley. He was living there at the time she removed there with her mother. She had not had any words with her husband about Fletcher. Her husband appeared to take as much notice of the child she had before she was married to him as of the other. She did not tell him on the 12th of June that she had come to live near someone who cared more for her than he did. Nothing of the kind was said. She did not in any way refer to Fletcher. The husband of Mrs Fletcher, from whom the prisoner borrowed the money, was the uncle to the young man. While he remained in the garden, between half-past eleven and one o'clock, he was playing with the children. Mrs Fletcher was there when the shots were fired. Re-examined – Fletcher was married some years ago, and now living with his wife. Sarah Seal, wife of John Seal, of Greenwich, Ripley. She said she was the mother of the last witness. In February last witness went to Nottingham and brought her back to her own house where she and the children lived until the 12th of June. On that day the prisoner went to the house, and witness on meeting him at the door refused to let him enter. His wife went to the door and spoke to him, and also shook hands with him. Witness and her daughter remained at the door with him, and conversed with him. He asked her daughter to give him another chance, but she refused. They accused him of borrowing money from Mrs Fletcher, which he denied, and she was sent for. Mrs Fletcher informed them that she had lent him money on different occasions. While she was there prisoner asked his wife again to go and live with him. His wife said she dare not, and would sooner go to the workhouse. Witness replied "You will not have to go there, as you have a good mother and father to help you." Directly afterwards she heard a shot, and saw her daughter fall. After that witness heard another shot, and was also shot. She fell, and on looking up saw the prisoner pointing the revolver towards the door. Witness then became unconscious. Cross-examined – Witness had seen a good deal of Spick after his marriage with her daughter. He was given to drinking, but had not drunk more heavily lately. He did not seem very excited when he was told about borrowing money from Mrs Fletcher. Witness did not taunt him with borrowing money from Mrs Fletcher. The young man named Fletcher was not mentioned. Nothing was said about her daughter while at Greenwich being near those who cared more for her than her husband. Re-examined – Mrs Fletcher formerly lodged with the prisoner and his wife, and had not paid her last week's board because, as she said. Prisoner owed her money. Harriett Fletcher, wife of James Fletcher, Old Radford, Nottingham, Said that in the latter part of 1882 she was lodging with the prisoner and his wife. In June she went on a visit to her sister, who lived at Greenwich, Ripley. On the 12th of June she was sent for to Mrs Seal's house. When she got there Mrs Seal, Mrs Spick, and the prisoner were standing at the door. Prisoner's wife asked if she had ever lent the prisoner any money, and she replied that she had on several occasions. Prisoner called her a liar. He then asked his little girl (Minnie) to go and fetch him a light to light his pipe. She did so. He then said something to his wife, but witness did not hear what it was. Directly afterwards she heard reports of a firearm, and saw Mrs Spick and Mrs Seal fall to the ground. He then went down the garden, after which he turned round and pointed the pistol at the witness. Mary Butler, living at Greenwich, Ripley, said her house was next door to Mrs Seal's. On the 12th of June prisoner went to her house, and for a drink of water, which she gave him. She thought he looked different from usual, and felt terrified. When he had gone out she locked the door. Directly after that she heard two shots fired, and the prisoner went again to her door, which he tried to force open. He was unable to do so, and went away. She then went to Mrs Seal's house, Where she saw Mrs Spick and Mrs Seal bleeding. Cross – examined - The prisoner's looks frightened witness.

Charles Smith, a porter at Ripley Co-operative stores, said that on the afternoon of June 12th he was passing Mrs Seal's house, when he saw the prisoner trying to open Mrs Butler's door. He looked very wild, and witness told him he thought he had been doing something he ought not to have done. Prisoner said he had not, it was another man. Witness did not know what had occurred then. Witness followed him into the Jessop's Arms public house. He went into the kitchen, but Mrs Clarke put him out, and witness then laid hold of him and put him in the bar. Mrs Clarke gave the prisoner two glasses of whiskey. Witness went outside the door which he locked. Directly afterwards he heard Mrs Clarke scream, the door was opened by a man named Hepworth, and Mrs Clarke showed witness a revolver , which she said she had taken from the prisoner, Prisoner then rushed into the kitchen and seized a knife, which he was putting up too his throat, when witness went behind him and took it from him. Cross-examined – He appeared very wild all the time. Thomas Glover, painter, of Dunkirk, Lenton, near Nottingham said he known the prisoner 16 or 17 years. Prisoner had told witness he should go to Ripley to see his wife and ask for the children. If she refused to see him he would put some lead through his wife and mother-in-law, witness thought he was joking. Cross-examined – Prisoner always seemed very fond of the children, and was constantly talking of going over to see them. David Taylor, Nottingham, said that on the night of June 11th prisoner slept at his house, which he left about quarter to eight. When he was going away he told witness that if anyone came to inquire for him he was to say he had left. He further said he should be back at night. Cross-examined – Prisoner slept in the same room as witness. John Wigley, assistant to Mr Jackson, Church Street, Nottingham, said the prisoner went to the shop on the 8th of June, and said he wanted to buy a revolver, as he was going to America. Witness sold him a revolver, of Belgian make, and also a number of cartridges. He identified the revolver produced. Arthur Holmes, Gregory Street, Lenton, Nottingham, said on the 11th of June he and the prisoner had a walk down Trent Lane. Prisoner produced a revolver from his pocket and fired it at a gate post. Witness also fired with the revolver. Prisoner told witness he was going to Liverpool the next day and intended to embark for New York. By His Lordship – He stood about ten yards from the gate post, at which he fired several times. It was an oak post and the bullets stuck in it. Police constable Eastaff said that on the 12th of June he was sent for to the Jessop's Arms, Ripley, where he found the prisoner, who was being held by Smith and Needham. Witness handcuffed him. Prisoner said "Let me have a drink for the last time." Witness declined to do so. He then charged the prisoner with wilfully shooting his wife and mother-in-law, but made no reply. On the way to the lock up he said "I don't know what I am doing; what is the charge?" Prisoner seemed excited. Inspector Cooke, of Ripley, spoke to receiving the revolver at the Jessop's Arms. He examined it finding four chambers loaded, and two empty chambers. He also received two cartridges from Needham. He afterwards went to the house of Mrs Seal, where he found part of a bullet and some blood on the floor. Witness subsequently went to the lock up and charged the prisoner with shooting at his wife and mother with intent to murder them. He asked "Are they dead?" and was told they were not. When witness was taking prisoner to Langley Mill, he again asked if the women were dead, and said that if they got better he should think he should not get more than 20 years. Mr Allen, surgeon, of Ripley, said that on the 12th of June, he was sent for to the house of Mrs Seal. He found Mrs Spick on a Chair in the yard. She was bleeding from a wound behind the ear, He could not detect anything in the wound at the time, but in a fortnight afterwards he discovered a bullet in the muscle of the neck, where it still remained. At present he had not thought it necessary to interfere with the bullet. She was ill a fortnight, and when he first saw her he thought she was in a dangerous condition. By his advice depositions were taken. He found Mrs Seal sitting on a chair in the yard. She had a wound in the cheek and another wound behind the ear. He ascertained there was a communication between the wounds. That in the cheek was the inlet and the outlet was behind the ear. She believed the bullet struck her cheek bone, which probably affected the shape of the bullet. Mrs Seal was ill about a fortnight. She was in danger the first day, and her depositions were taken. Cross-examined – The affection described by the wife appeared to be a local attack of paralysis. All paralysis did not affect the brain. Mr Weightman then addressed the jury on behalf of the prisoner. He said he was fully aware that any sympathy which existed in court was not with the prisoner in the bar. He should, therefore, have to address to the jury such remarks as were warranted by the evidence. Before they convicted the prisoner of the charge against him they would have to be sure that he intended to take his wife's life. It would, therefore, be necessary for them to carefully watch the facts of the case. It might be what the prisoner said to Arthur Holmes and to Wigley with reference to emigrating to America was absolutely true, and that he bought the revolver to take with him, for it is well known that persons usually took firearms with them when they went to a foreign country. It might be that on the 12th of June prisoner went to Ripley without any wicked desire in his mind. It had been proved that he was passionately fond of his children, whom he was constantly talking about, and probably went to his mother-in-law's house to have a last look at them, and to make a last appeal to his wife to go and live with him again. If he intended to take his wife's life, as suggested by the prosecution, why did he not do it immediately he had purchased the weapon? There was no expression of vindictiveness on going to the house, and it might have been that having been taunted with having borrowed money from Mrs Fletcher, the name suggested the young man to his mind who had wronged his wife, and in a hasty moment he drew the revolver, but not with the intention of committing murder.

His Lordship, in summing up, said the prisoner was charged with wounding his wife with intent to murder her, and also with wounding her with the intention of doing her grievous bodily harm. It was for the jury to honestly discharge their duty by deciding from the evidence whether the prisoner was guilty of the first or second charges, or not guilty of either. They would have to decide whether the prisoner, when he pulled the trigger of the revolver, intended to murder his wife. It was not necessary to decide that he had that intention when he bought the weapon, although it seemed to him that if a man fired a pistol with the intention of shooting at another person he must take the consequences of his act, if the bullet struck a vital part and death ensued. The jury after deliberating a few momments, returned a verdict of guilty of wounding his wife with the intent to murder her. His Lordship then passed sentence, He said the prisoner stood very properly convicted of shooting his wife with intent to murder her. He could not but think it was almost a miracle that he was not standing in the dock convicted of the crime of wilful murder. If his wife or mother-in-law had died he would undoubtedly have expiated his crime on the scaffold. He had, however, been found guilty of a crime nearest to that of wilful murder. He intended it, but happily no life had been lost. He (His Lordship) had considered whether it was not his bounded duty to pass the severest sentence which could be past next to death, which was penal servitude for life. Although he had not decided to do that, the sentence he intended to pass was within an ace of penal servitude for life. It was somewhat shorter than that, but it was that of twenty years penal servitude.

FURTHER INFORMATION

The 1881 Census revealed Thomas Spick and Ann Spick along with Harriet Fletcher (Lodger) who two years later would be a witness at the trial were living at 13 Mount street, Nottingham. On the 30th of July 1883 Thomas Robert Spick was sentenced to 20 years penal servitude for attempted murder and arrived at Pentonville Prison on the 13th of August. On his admission to the prison Thomas complained of great pains in his head and was suffering discharge from one of his ears and he also notified the prison he was paralysed in one side of his face. By the 20th of August Thomas was admitted to hospital and passed away on the 24th of August 1883 aged 27, just 25 days after his conviction. A post-mortem examination revealed a hole through the skull from the ear, there being a large abscess on the brain. Otherwise the body was generally healthy. Ann married again in 1886 and with her second husband had at least six more children.

Sources: 1881 Census, Islington Gazette 29th August 1883, England & Wales Birth, Marriage, and Death 1837-1983 records.

HOUSE STRUCK BY LIGHTNING AT HEAGE

DERBYSHIRE TIMES, SATURDAY JULY 7TH 1883

A severe thunderstorm passed over Heage on Wednesday afternoon, and a house at Heage was struck by the lightning. A bed ridden old woman named Fox had a narrow escape. The roof of the house was partly torn off by the fluid which passed down the chimney, shattered a window, knocked plaster off the walls, and broke a quantity of crockery.

THE STORM AT RIPLEY

During the storm on Wednesday afternoon the farm house of Mr Joseph Green, (the Hollybush Farm), was stuck by lightning. One of the bricks in the gable end was displaced, and the roof considerably damaged. Mr Green and two of his children, who were in the kitchen at the time, were struck by lightning, but were not seriously hurt. On Street Lane near Ripley, one of the hailstones was picked up and was found to weigh exactly one ounce. Damage was done to fruit trees and potatoes.

LANDLADY STRUCK AT NORTH WINGFIELD

At North Wingfield on Wednesday night the lightning struck the White Hart Inn. Mrs Allen, wife of the landlord, her son and the servant girl, who were in the bar were knocked down. Mrs Allen lost the use in one side. Dr Lee, of Clay Cross, was called in, and hopes that the use of the disabled side will be restored. Mrs Allen was a little better on Thursday. The house is not much damaged.

PROPOSED NEW RAILWAY
AND STATION RIPLEY

THE DERBY DAILY TELEGRAPH
SATURDAY NOVEMEBER 17TH 1883

MIDLAND RAILWAY EXTENSION. – A plan has been issued of the proposed Midland line of railway through Ripley. It is proposed to come from Pentrich across Alma and Outram streets. The Station is marked to be placed near the Jessop Arms on the Nottingham road. The line will probably unite with the Butterley line. The project is very favourably received.

TRAGEDY AT WILLIAM IV INN RIPLEY

DERBYSHIRE ADVERTISER AND JOURNAL
FRIDAY NOVEMBER 19TH 1886

Last Sunday morning the neighbourhood of Lowes Hill, Ripley was greatly excited by the reports that Mr Cornelius Jenkins, landlord of the King William IV Inn, Ripley had shot himself and his wife. This proved to be correct, the unfortunate man dying almost immediately. Mrs Jenkins was wounded in the breast, but it is hoped her injuries will not prove serious. The sad affair is the principal topic of conversation in Ripley. An inquest was held at the above Inn on Monday evening last, before Mr W H Whiston, coroner, and a jury composed of the following persons: - Messers T M Thrush (foreman), I Machin, J Oldershaw, F Payne, T Moon, J Adams, J Tealby, W Redfern, E T Baker, J Elliott, M Gregory, and W Hawkins. At the commencement of the proceedings the coroner decided to take the evidence of Mrs Jenkins in her bedroom, where she at present compelled to remain, being under medical treatment. In the presence of the coroner and jury the following evidence was given by the wife of the deceased: - The body just viewed by the jury is that of my late husband. He was a licensed victualler, and kept this house. He was 57 years of age. We were at home on Sunday. I was in the little kitchen about 11am. My husband was in the same room. He stood with his back to the window, his right hand was by the door, and his left by the fireplace. My little granddaughter was in the same room. I was sitting on the sofa, mixing the dinner for the pigs. I told my granddaughter to go and see what time it was in the next room. The moment she left the room he pulled his right hand from the back of him. I saw he had something in his hand. He fired one shot I said "oh!" and moved slightly. It struck me on the arm, and rebounding made two holes in my dress. He fired again quickly, and I was struck in the right breast. I jumped up and ran into the other room, and said "Oh, run and fetch someone; I shall bleed to death." As I ran out of my room I heard the report of two shots, one after the other, from the kitchen. I came into the passage, and out of the front door. I saw my husband's head just in the doorway, on the floor. I knew he had fired at me with a six chambered revolver. It was five minutes before any help came. There was only my little granddaughter and servant in the house. He looked at me three minutes before he fired at me. He had been very disagreeable in the early morning of Sunday. He did not get to bed till 3 o'clock on Sunday morning. He had been troubled by reading about the death of Archer. We had had no actual quarrel. Deceased was also troubled about money matters, and had often threatened to blow out my brains when in drink. He had been drinking lately. We have been married thirty eight years. He always said we should die together. – George Gaunt said he was going down Lowes hill at 11:45 am on Sunday last, when he saw a girl run up the road, and heard somebody say, "Fetch the police." Just then Mrs Jenkins came to the front door, and witness saw blood running down the front of her dress. She said, "He has shot me and shot himself." Witness went into the house, and saw deceased with his head against the door and lying on the floor of the passage near the settle. He looked at deceased and called him by name, but made no reply, and immediately breathed his last. He was bleeding from his mouth. Witness noticed a revolver lying at his feet, which he picked up and showed to some of the company present. He then went for the police, the son of the deceased, and the Doctor. Witness knew the deceased very well. He never spoke after he fired the fatal shots. – Police constable Bradwell, of Ripley, went to the above named house and saw deceased lying on the floor of the passage, and blood was on the floor near him. He had the body removed into the house. Witness then examined and found a hole in the wall made by a bullet, and also found part of a bullet on the settle. He noticed a revolver near his feet. Upon examination of the body he saw deceased was injured about his mouth, from which blood was flowing. The left eye was black, and a bruise on the right temple. The black eye might be caused by his falling against the wooden partition, and the discoloured state of his face on the left side might, perhaps, be accounted for by his falling on the rough and uneven bricks on the floor. Amongst other things found in the possession of the deceased was a diary kept by himself, and containing the following entry: - "Nov 14, At home now with mistress; called me terribly. Miserable life since marriage. God help me." Witness searched the drawer and found a box of ball cartridges, of which 37 were loaded, and 6 discharged. The witness had in his possession the under bodice of Mrs Jenkins, which was stained with blood, and had two holes in it, made evidently by the bullets which deceased fire at her, as stated in her evidence. – This was the whole of the statement made by the witnesses, after which the CORONER summed up briefly, and said the only question for the jury to decide was as to the state of mind deceased was in when he committed suicide. – After a short deliberation, the jury returned a verdict to the effect "deceased committed suicide by shooting himself with a revolver during temporary insanity." – Mr Jenkins was well known in Ripley as a steady man, and attentive to his business. He was employed at Ripley factory, and also a public accountant. He formerly kept the Thorn Tree Hotel, Waingroves, Ripley, and the George Inn, Hartshay, Ripley. He had only just come to the place where he finished his career. Mrs Jenkins has received a serious shock to her system, but it is hoped the injuries will not prove serious. The tragedy has been, and continues to be, staple topic of conversation in Ripley.

The King William nursing home, formerly the King William IV Inn, Ripley photographed in 2023. (Authors Collection)

THE QUEENS JUBILEE CELEBRATIONS

THE DERBY MERCURY
WEDNESDAY JUNE 29TH 1887

The streets of Alfreton were gaily decked with flags and banners, and festoons of evergreens. The children of the day and Sunday schools were regaled with tea at their respective schoolrooms, and the aged were entertained at dinner at the Town Hall. In the afternoon at four o'clock the children assembled in the High street, where hymns were sung. A procession was formed, headed by the members of the local board and Alfreton Brass Band, to the new Recreation Ground, which has been secured in honour of the Jubilee, was reached. On arriving at the ground Mr Morewood unlocked the gate, which was opened by MR T Willgoose, the chairman of the Local Board, amidst great cheering. In the centre of the ground a platform had been erected, and from it Mrs Palmer-Morewood formally declared the ground open, after which Mr Palmer-Morewood offered a few words of hearty congratulation. Mr Willgoose also declared the ground properly open. The proceedings were concluded by singing and the offering up of prayer by the vicar (the rev W H Draper). Afterwards the children went into Alfreton Park, where athletic sports took place.

BELPER

The inhabitants were awakened from their slumbers by the continuous booming of cannon fired in the meadows, and by eight o'clock the streets were thronged with people. It was not decided to publicly celebrate the Jubilee in Belper until the eleventh hour, but when steps were taken for a general rejoicing the movement promised to be a great success. A committee was formed of which Capt Strutt was president, and the Revs F Knowles and C Cowen were Hon secretaries, and subscriptions came in freely, amounting to nearly £150. It was arranged for all aged people in the town to be provided with a good dinner, and all the children were given a medal and were entertained to tea at their respective schools, the committee allowing 5d per head for each child. A thanksgiving service was held in St Peter's Church. At two o'clock the united schools met in the Market place, where close upon 3,000 children sang special hymns. Three bands had been engaged. The scholars afterwards adjourned to their respective schools, and after tea sports were provided in the meadows.

CODNOR

For its size Codnor may be said to have done its part in celebrating the Jubilee of Her Majesty. A committee representing the various inhabitants, under the direction of Mr W Taylor, made preparations on an elaborate scale. Subscriptions were collected sufficient to enable the committee to provide tea free for every boy and girl under 16 years of age, to every man and woman over 68 years of age, and to the deserving poor. About 1500 persons had tea in a large field, kindly lent for the purpose. Before tea a large meeting was held in the Market place, presided over by Mr W Taylor. An address was given by Mr T Farnsworth. Mr W Eyre also addressed the meeting. At the close a procession was formed at the Cemetery, where a Jubilee oak was planted by Mrs Middleton, widow of the late vicar. After this ceremony tea was provided, and subsequently sports and fireworks.

GOLDEN VALLEY

On Jubilee day Mrs Briddon, landlady of the Newlands Hotel, gave a dinner to seventy poor people. The next day the same benevolent lady gave a free tea to eighty-four poor woman, and the following day gave a free tea to 150 children. The village was decorated with flags and garlands.

HEANOR

On Tuesday at Heanor the festivities commemorative of Her Majesty's Jubilee were of a very imposing character. During Monday the inhabitants were busy engaged in decorating their houses, and at as early an hour as four o'clock on Tuesday morning bands of singers were heard in the streets singing the National Anthem. The friendly societies of the district assembled in the Market place, and, headed by the Hucknall Huthwaite and Heanor Brass Bands walked in procession through the streets, subsequently proceeding to the parish church, where Rev C E L Corfield delivered an address. A mass meeting numbering 5000 persons, was then held on the green in front of the Wesleyan Chapel, where special hymns were sung by 2460 children. Mr T Mayfield presided and addresses were delivered by

Red Lion Square, Heanor around the time of the Queen's Jubilee celebrations. (Authors Collection)

the Rev C E L Corfield and the Rev G Avis. Subsequently a procession was formed, and the people afterwards partook of tea at the different schools, the friendly societies having dinner at their lodge rooms. The old and poor people of the parish had a substantial treat, the cost of which was defrayed by public subscription. At least 550 persons sat down in the Town Hall and other rooms in connection with the public offices. Over £97 was subscribed for Jubilee purposes, and after the present arrangements have been carried out about £40 will be left towards erecting something of a permanent nature. The following ladies presided at the tables and attended to the wants of the old people : - Mrs Mayfield, Mrs Burton, Miss Corfield, Miss Burton, Mrs Towson, Mrs Woolley, Mrs G Oldenshaw, Mrs Robinson, Mrs Thorpe, Mrs Bonner, Mrs Prince, Mrs Hicking, Mrs Brown, Miss Eagle, and others. After tea the hall was packed to excess with the old people, and a programme of music was gone through. The National Anthem was sung at the commencement, and at the close votes of thanks to the committee and ladies who presided the tables, together with the chairman was heartily accorded. On Saturday the Jubilee festivities were continued at Heanor. During the afternoon the Heanor Brass Band played selections of music in Red Lion square, and at four o'clock proceeded to Messers L and R Morley's factory, where a large room had been gaily decorated. Here over 600 persons sat down to a ham tea, subsequently adjourning to the Heanor Hall grounds, where sports and pastimes were heartily entered into. Mr J Fletcher, lace manufacturer, West valley, generously gave tea to all his workmen and their wives and children, a very enjoyable evening being spent. Messers Bryan Brothers, lace manufacturers, Heanor gate, gave a similar treat to their employees.

ILKESTON

The rejoicing were conducted under the auspices of the Town Council, which met in the morning and agreed to an address to the Queen, and also sent a congratulatory telegram from the only borough created in the Jubilee year. The town was gaily decorated from end to end. The Mayor and Corporation, accompanied by the members of the School Board, the officials of the corporation, the various Dissenting ministers, the Ilkeston Fire Brigade, and the local detachment of the Derbyshire Volunteers, and members of the Engine smith's Association, together with a small force of police, attended a divine service at the parish church at noon. The Sunday school scholars of the town assembled in the Market place at the close of the service in the presence of the Mayor and Corporation, and sang a number of hymns under the direction of Mr Wm Gadsby. The schools then dispersed to their various rooms, where tea was provided. The adult population were provided with a free fete and gala on the Recreation Ground, which was attended by a large crowd of persons. The Ilkeston Brass Band and the Cossall Brass Band took part in the proceedings. In the evening the Town Hall was brilliantly illuminated. A large number of sheep were roasted in different parts of the town and distributed amongst the people. The expenses of the celebration have been met by public subscriptions, over £200, having been subscribed. On Saturday Mr Holding, the manager of Cossall Colliery, gave a dinner to all employees of the company, and tea to their wives, some 500 men and 300 women being entertained.

LANGLEY MILL

On Tuesday the Sunday school Union at Langley Mill held their first annual treat, when the united schools of General Baptists, Wesleyans, Free Church, and Primitive Methodists, formed in procession, and headed by the Langley Mill Brass Band, paraded the streets, afterwards the school children had tea at their chapels. Games and amusements took place. All the old people, to the number of about 200, were treated to a free dinner and tea in the Cooperative Hall, the expenses being defrayed by public subscription.

RIPLEY

On Tuesday last there was a large gathering of the inhabitants of Ripley together with the various Sunday schools in the Market place in celebration of her Majesty's accession. Mr W J Cooper presided, and in his opening remarks said that this vast gathering of the inhabitants and all the Sunday schools of Ripley, with the liberal response for funds proved that they were in deepest sympathy with this Jubilee day, and that no more loyal hearts beat than theirs; and as the bells were ringing on this never to be forgotten day over the country we love as well, may they "ring in the nobler modes of life." The first Derbyshire Rifle Volunteers, under the direction of Major Corfield, were present. The Rev C R Round, in a few appropriate words, announced the National Anthem, which was sung right heartily. At the word of command by Major Corfield the volunteers fired a feu de joie, after which the band played the National Anthem. Captain Crossley then proposed three cheers for the Queen, which were given. Prayer was then offered by the Rev W Calladine, followed by a very suitable address by the Rev W E Bradstock, vicar of Ripley, in which he pointed out the great blessings we enjoy under the reign of Her Majesty. Major Corfield then proposed that the respectful congratulations of this assembly be sent to the Queen, which was seconded by Mr W B Bembridge, and carried by acclamation. The chairman issued this message to Her Majesty shortly afterwards. The Rev F Jones gave out the second hymn, after which the vicar pronounced the Benediction. Mr A Day acted as marshal in a very efficient manner. All the Sunday school children had tea provided in their respective school rooms, and then adjourned to a field for games. A free tea was given to over 700 poor people and children in the Town Hall. In the evening there were sports, fireworks, balloons and a large bonfire in a field off Cromford road.

SWANWICK

The village was gaily decorated with arches and garlands, and the school children marched to the grounds at Swanwick Hayes, where they had tea and various amusements.

STREET LANE

A free tea was given in the schoolroom on Jubilee day to 200 persons. After tea games were resorted to in a field lent by Mr J Butler. All Children under sixteen years and adults over sixty years were presented with medals.

MAN IN ILKESTON CLAIMS TO BE JACK THE RIPPER

BELPER AND ALFRETON CHRONICLE
SATURDAY OCTOBER 13TH 1888

A Local "JACK THE RIPPER" – A seedy looked individual rejoicing in the now notorious title of "Jack the Ripper," or as he was entered on the charge sheet, John Rip, alias Wynne, alias Smith, was brought up to custody charged with being drunk and disorderly at Ilkeston on Sunday night, and also with having stopped Priscilla Bennett and stolen a shilling from her on Friday night. – The young woman, who lives in Wheatley's Row, Ilkeston, alleges that she was stopped by a man in Burns street, Ilkeston, at the back of the Independent chapel, and robbed of a shilling under the threat of being "Whitechapelled." That night search was made through public houses and lodging houses of the town for the miscreant, but without success. On being arrested on Sunday night he asserted that he was Jack the Ripper, and threatened to shoot the police when he got his liberty again. When Miss Bennett was shown the prisoner she identified him as the man who robbed her. – Prisoner said he was innocent of the charge "before God and man." The young woman was swearing away his character. He could prove that he was in a public house at the time. – Remanded to Ilkeston on Thursday.

Burns Street Ilkeston in 2023. The Independent chapel on the left is now a private residence. (Authors Collection)

FURTHER INFORMATION

On being found guilty of stealing 1s from Priscilla Bennett and receiving a sentence of 3 months in gaol with hard labour, John Rip as the prisoner was known replied "I'll do it, then blow her brains out afterwards."

Sources: Derbyshire advertiser and Journal October 19th 1888

MIDNIGHT NAN THEFTS - HEANOR

THE DERBY MERCURY
WEDNESDAY JANUARY 23RD 1889

Considerable excitement was caused in the vicinity of Mount Street, Heanor, about nine o'clock on Friday night. For some time past, the neighbourhood has been annoyed by repeated thefts of coal but no clue could be obtained of the thieves. About the timed named, Mrs Arthur Smith heard footsteps and rumbling in the entry. She found Ann Bailey, 60 years of age, of Calladine House, commonly known at Heanor as "Midnight Nan," with a huge lump of coal wrapped up in a cloth, and just in the act of running off with it. On being questioned by the owners, Bailey said she had the coal given to her, but was forbidden naming the party who gave it. Mrs Smith identified the lump of coal as hers. Persisting her innocence, "Midnight Nan," who is a well-known character, was placed in the hands of the police constable Marshall and charged her with theft, but indignantly replied, "You know me too well, Mr Marshall to do such a thing." Ultimately she was conveyed to the Langley Mill lock up.

REMARKBLE DEATH BY LIGHTNING
AT CODNOR

DERBYSHIRE ADVERTISER AND JOURNAL
FRIDAY MAY 31ST 1889

An inquest was held at the Lord Byron Inn, Codnor, on Friday, before Mr Whiston, coroner, on the body of Ann Tagg . – Hannah Matkin said the deceased was a widow, and 80 years of age. She lived alone, and witness saw her alive in the front bedroom cleaning the windows about 2:30pm on Thursday. Witness sent her son during the storm to call deceased but received no reply. She then went upstairs and found the deceased sitting in a chair. Witness shouted about three times to deceased, but receiving no answer she went to the grandson of the deceased and called him in. Witness noticed a strong smell of sulphur and smoke in the room where the deceased was sitting. – Dr R F Palmer deposed that a severe storm of thunder, lightning and rain passed over Codnor on Thursday last. The lightning was very vivid and he never saw it nearer to the ground. He was sent for to the residence of the deceased, when he found the air full of sulphur. He noticed the deceased in a chair, but did not suspect death, thinking it was only fright. He then examined the body, which was quite dead, and found a mark below the left breast, showing where she had been struck by the electric fluid, which must have gone through the heart and caused instant death. It then appeared to have passed out of the heart downwards, setting fire to the lower part of her clothing. Some false teeth worn by deceased fell out, and a pair of spectacles were found on the floor near to the body of the deceased. The chair on which she had been sitting was split, and considerable damage was done to the house. – The Coroner said it was evident from the testimony of Dr Palmer that deceased met her death by lightning, and a verdict to that effect was at once returned.

THE SWANWICK MURDERER

THE SHEFFIELD EVENING TELEGRAPH
WEDNESDAY AUGUST 21ST 1889

EXECUTION OF HORTON THIS MORNING

At eight o'clock this morning George Horton, who was convicted at the last Derbyshire Assizes for the murder of his daughter, Kate, aged 8 years, at Swanwick on the morning of Monday, the 20th May, was hung within the precincts of the Derby Gaol. Berry was the Executioner.

THE EXECUTION
SPECIAL TELEGRAM

At eight o'clock this morning within the precincts of Derby Gaol, George Horton, collier, Swanwick, was executed for poisoning his little daughter to obtain insurance money on her life. The execution was conducted privately, only Under-Sheriff, Prison Chaplin, Governor, doctors, and representatives of the Press being present. Berry, of Bradford, who officiated, arrived at the gaol yesterday afternoon. An immense crowd assembled outside the prison, and placed themselves near to the open space where the execution was conducted. The bell commenced toiling at a quarter to eight, and then the procession to the condemned cell was made, where Horton was pinioned. He was extremely nervous and dejected. The sentence was carried out punctually to time, and when the black flag was hoisted there was dead silence amongst the crowd, who quietly dispersed when they knew the last scene was over. Since his condemnation Horton has occupied a cell next to the infirmary, and has been under medical treatment, his health having given way under the extreme excitement and worry. He was visited by the Rev J E Matthews, vicar of Swanwick, to whom he first made a confession on three different occasions, and has also been frequently instructed and prayed for and read to by the Rev C C Crelin, the prison chaplin. Since his confession he has appeared very attentive to the religious instruction imparted, and has spent a good deal of time in reading and praying, the Bible being a constant companion, and he has appeared very penitent. He has had interviews with thirteen different persons, including his children from Belper Workhouse and others who are earning their own living, his mother in law, several relatives by marriage, and Boushill, one of the principal witnesses at the trial, and the Rev J E Matthews, who last saw him on Monday. He spent the whole of Tuesday in reading and praying, and at night wrote five letters, making 24 letters written by him in gaol. The five letters were written to relatives bidding them farewell, and urging them to become religious and shun drink. He retired to bed about the usual hour, eight o'clock on Tuesday night, and slept very soundly, having to be awakened this morning at a quarter to six. He then rose, and after washing himself took a walk in the gaol grounds for 20 minutes, and appeared to be fairly cheerful. He then ate a good breakfast, consisting of bread and butter and tea. At twenty minutes to seven the chaplain, Rev C C Crelin, entered the cell, where the prisoner had spent some time previously in praying and reading. The chaplain remained with him till the end, the time being spent in devotion, but the convict did not allude to the crime or make any other statement concerning it. Shortly before eight o'clock the condemned man left his cell in the care of two wardens, being met at the door by the Under-sheriff and other officials, and he was pinioned without any resistance in the courtyard by Berry. The procession then moved forward to the scaffold, the chaplain meanwhile reciting the burial service of the Church of England, Horton audibly responding. On being placed on the scaffold, to which he walked firmly, although he seemed very nervous, he commenced praying. His voice trembled and became almost inaudible. Just as he had fervently uttered the words "Lord have mercy upon my soul," Berry raised the lever and the drop fell. There was scarcely any vibration and death was instantaneous. Directly the drop fell the black flag hoisted over the prison walls to announce that all was over. It was a new scaffold with a 6ft drop. Horton weighed 10st 4lb, and was 5ft 3in high. The inquest was subsequently held by Mr Whiston, county coroner, and the body was buried in the prison grounds, that grave being next to that in which Delany was buried a year ago.

HISTORY OF THE CRIME

The history of the crime as detailed to Justice Hawkins, showed that Horton resided at Swanwick, near Alfreton. He was a widower, had six children, and was employed at the Alfreton New Colliery. Two of his children were away, and four lived at home. In the same house as the Hortons lived a family named Bowskill. The latter occupied bedrooms which were separate from those of the Hortons, but the two families used the same living room. The murdered child, Kate Horton, who was eight years old and slept with her brother Joseph and her father; the other children having a bed in another room upstairs. On the evening of Sunday, the 19th of May, Kate went to chapel, and when she returned home she was taken to bed. Her elder sister, Sarah Jane, 13 years of age, retired about 10 o'clock, and Horton himself went shortly afterwards. What took place during the night, if anything, is not known, but early on the Monday morning, as was their custom, the Bowskills knocked at the wall which divided their bedroom from Horton's for the purpose of waking Sarah Jane, who generally got up and lightened the fire. This morning however, Horton was first to get up, and while he was dressing, Sarah Jane heard her sister Kate say to her father "Dadda, I want a drink." Horton replied that he was in a hurry and had not time to get one for her; if she wanted one she must go down and get one for herself. Directly afterwards Horton passed through the bedroom occupied by Sarah Jane and the other children, and proceeding downstairs left the house. After he had gone the girl Sarah Jane dropped asleep, but she was awakened very shortly by the deceased, who went to her, and complaining of a pain in her inside, threw herself on the bed and moaned as if she were in intense agony. As the child did not get better a neighbour was sent for and all that could be done for her was done, but she died about seven o'clock, or some hour and a half after her father left her. Before she died deceased was asked if she had taken anything, and she said her father had given her some blue stuff out of a bottle. When it was found that the child could not live, Mr Bowskill went to the Alfreton New Colliery to inform the father of the fact, but he was surprised to learn Horton had not been to work. He, therefore, returned to Swanwick, and on getting there found Horton had arrived before him. Inquiries afterwards showed that Horton, after leaving home, went towards the pit, but on reaching Alfreton he appears to have turned off the main road, and retraced his steps to Swanwick by the way of a footpath through the fields. When nearing his home one of his children went out and met him, and told him that his daughter Kate was dead. At first he appeared unconcerned, but on seeing the corpse of the child he kissed it and dropped a tear or two on the little face. The statement of the deceased that her father had given her something from a bottle, and the fact that while she was dying the child clenched her hands, twitched her eyes and mouth, while her legs were quite stiff, caused Mrs Bowskill to look about for signs of poison, but although she looked carefully, she could find none. There were only three cups in the house, and all these were free from any such signs. A few days after the death of his daughter Horton made application to Dr John Joseph Bingham for a death certificate, but the gentleman refused to give him one, and his request that Mr John Wiles, the Swanwick agent of the Refuge Assurance Company, would pay him £7, for which the life of his daughter was insured, was likewise unsuccessful. The circumstances of the case pointed so strongly to Horton being the murderer of his child that he was arrested by the police, and he was eventually committed for trial on the capital charge both by the local bench of magistrates and the coroner's jury. At the hearing at the assizes the prosecution was conducted by Mr Etherington Smith, with whom was Mr Garratt, while at the request of Justice Hawkins Mr Appleton watched the case on behalf of the prisoner. Witnesses were called who bore out the above statement, and Dr Bingham spoke to making the post mortem examination and sending various parts of the body to Mr Allen, the analyst. The latter found in the parts sent eight-tenths of a grain of strychnine. Allowing for the amount that would have been absorbed by the system, he gave it as his opinion that the little child had had no less than two grains given to her. He also found a bluish substance in the stomach and intestines which pointed to the fact that the strychnine had been in vermin powder. He stated that half a grain of strychnine would be a fatal dose to a child the age of deceased. After the whole of the evidence had been taken, Mr Smith, for the Crown, could only make one suggestion, and that was that Horton gave his child a quantity of vermin powder, and that his object in murdering her was to obtain the £7 insurance money. He argued that if Horton had not administered the powder who had? It was not likely that the child would take it herself. Everything pointed to the fact that Horton had murdered the child. There was no trace left of the poison, and Horton was not able to go to work, but was restless, and had to return home to ascertain whether his work had had its desired effect. Mr Appleton followed, and admitted that if Horton had committed this crime for the paltry sum of £7 he had been guilty of one of the foulest and most cruel crimes that could take place. He, However, thought that such a conclusion was altogether contrary to the teaching of nature, and he pleaded with the jury before they found the father guilty of this terrible deed to weigh the evidence over very carefully, and if there was a doubt in their minds to give his client the benefit of it. Justice Hawkins then summed up the whole case. He carefully went through the evidence, and then fairly dealt with the arguments advanced by Mr Appleton for the accused man. The jury were only absent twenty five minutes, and they returned a verdict which not only proved to be right, but which was concurred in by nearly everyone who had heard the trial. In passing the death sentence his

Lordship, amidst breathless silence, implored Horton to make good use of the few hours left to him on earth. He had been guilty of a cruel crime, of a deed almost too horrible to contemplate; he had broken God's law, and he entreated him to make peace with him while he yet remained on earth. Horton listened to the sentence with perfect calmness, and did not exhibit the slightest emotion, calling out when being led from the dock that he was innocent. While he has been confined in the condemned cell, however, the ministrations of the chaplain have had a marked effect on him, and he has admitted his guilt and the justice of the sentence which was passed upon him.

TROTTING MATCH FOR £20 FROM CLAY CROSS TO ALFRETON

THE SHEFFIELD DAILY TELEGRAPH SATURDAY JANUARY 11TH 1890

Considerable excitement was evidenced in Clay Cross on Thursday afternoon to witness a trotting match from the Queen's Head Inn, Clay Cross to the George Inn, Alfreton, for £20, between Mr John Cupit's Jim and Mr Henry Hill's Tommy, owners to drive. The betting was in favour of Jim, who after the first mile, had the race in hand, Tommy refusing to pass the public houses on the way without a call, and at Shirland his owner seeing he had no chance gave up.

NEW LINE FROM RIPLEY TO HEANOR

THE DERBY MERCURY, WEDNESDAY JUNE 4TH 1890

The first train from Ripley to Codnor and Heanor via Ambergate, at nine o'clock on Monday morning came into the Ripley station at the appointed time. There was a large number of spectators present to witness the arrival. Several persons left by the train from Ripley for the purpose of having a ride and nothing more. On Arrival of the train at Codnor the railway bridge was crowded with spectators and the greatest interest was manifested.

Some of the oldest inhabitants got into the train at Codnor station apparently much pleased at living so long as to see a railway to Codnor. A number of school children got in at Codnor, for whom tickets could not be obtained, a sufficient number not having been provided. The next proceeded to Heanor, where some hundreds of persons had assembled to witness novel proceedings. The return train at 9.54 to Ripley was again crowded. The Codnor and Heanor stations are both neat and commodious, and there is no doubt the branch line will pay the directors for the immense outlay they have made. The new line was duly inspected on Saturday last, as is usual in such cases. An excellent service of trains has been arranged, and travellers from Chesterfield and the North instead of having to journey to Derby and then come back again a short distance and proceed along the Ripley branch will have two routes open to them. They may travel either by Pye Bridge or Ambergate, thence along the Butterley branch, and then by the new Ripley and Heanor line. The service of trains arranged on the following simple system : - Starting from Mansfield a train will run to Pye Bridge, thence to Butterley, then, branching off to the left to Ripley, go forward through Crosshill and Codnor to Heanor. Then it will run back from Heanor through Ripley to the Butterley branch and instead of going back to Pye Bridge and Mansfield – will go forward to Ambergate. From Ambergate the service will be exactly reversed, the trains after travelling to Ripley or Heanor running back to Pye Bridge and Mansfield. By this ingenious arrangement every place will be well served.

Ripley Station of the Midland Railway Company (Author's Collection)

CODNOR

THE NEW RAILWAY – Monday was a red-letter day in the history of the parish. All the inhabitants, old and young, turned out to welcome the arrival of the first passenger train, hundreds of people during the day availed themselves of the opportunity of taking a railway ride on the first day of its introduction into the place. The first train was one going in the direction of Heanor from Ripley, and quite a friendly competition took place as to who should purchase the first ticket issued at the station. Mr Farnworth had the honour to become the first purchaser. The authorities had not expected such a rush of passengers as proved to be the case, and in a very short time all the tickets for Heanor had been disposed of, and passengers had to travel without them. Mr Pine treated about 60 of his first-class scholars to a ride to Heanor, and later in the day Mrs Pine took whole of the girls under her care for a trip to Ripley.

Codnor and Crosshill Station of the Midland Railway Company
(Author's Collection)

A LION AT LARGE IN LANGLEY MILL

THE SHEFFIELD EVENING TELEGRAPH AND STAR
FRIDAY JULY 17TH 1891

GREAT EXCITEMENT

Great alarm was created on Wednesday night about 9.30 by the report that a lion was at large in the village. The animal escaped from a menagerie belonging to Biddale and Company, which was erected on a piece of wasteland by the side of the main road. The performance for the evening being nearly at a close the lion was expected to ride round the ring on the back of an elephant. It successfully completed the task, when the elephant drew up to the cage door as to allow the lion to enter. Not being thoroughly opposite the door the animal did not succeed in entering, but fell to the ground. The greatest consternation ensued amongst the spectators, who ran hither and tither for safety. While the lion, through fright or otherwise, escaped under the canvas. It made its way up Victoria terrace, and turned downed an entry, frightening everybody in its course. It then went across some gardens to land adjoining a wood-shop in the occupation of Mr Brough. The keepers here intercepted it, and with great caution managed to cover it with a net. It was then roped on either side for the safety of those deputed to convey it to its domicile. A considerable time elapsed before the animal was lodged in its cage, being very stubborn. The capture of the ferocious beast without injury to anyone is considered very fortunate, the same animal having attacked and injured one of the keepers very severely the night previous.

ASTON VILLA V HEANOR TOWN
FA CUP ROUND ONE

NOTTINGHAM EVENING POST
SATURDAY JANUARY 16TH 1892

The visit of Heanor Town to Perry Barr this afternoon was looked upon by the villans as a sort of walk over for them, and they went in for no special preparation for the match. Previous to Saturday, when they sustained such a bad defeat at Derby, the Heanor men, who had won 12 games in succession, and scored 53 goals to six, were rather confident that they would surprise the Villa men, but since that time they calmed down considerably, and when they made the journey to Birmingham today they were content to do their best to give the famous Perry Bar team a good game. The Villa were fully represented with the expectation of Brown, who was injured last Saturday, and Heanor also had the best available team in the field. There was a capital attendance. The ground, which was very hard, was covered with sand. The visitors won the toss, but there was nothing to gain in the choice of ends. Directly on starting the home team began to attack, and Carlin was soon found plenty of work to do. The Heanor custodian, however, was in great form, and he cleared grandly. Then the Heanor forwards dashed away, and twice was Warner's charge in jeopardy. After a long attack on Heanor's goal the visitors again get away finely, and Warner had to scoop away a long, low shot. The game still continued all in favour of the Villa, but they could not break through the defence. Again Heanor got away, and Warner had to save, though directly after Carlin was in turn called on. Corners fell to the Villa, but they could not get the ball through, and at half time neither team had scored. In the second half the Villa began to press, but though they kept swinging about in front of the Heanor goal they could not break through, Wright in particular doing any amount of clever things in goal. A couple of fouls to the visitors enabled them to relieve their lines, and they went to the other end but soon afterwards the Villa ran in and

Hodgetts scored. Pressing hard, the Villa scored again by Hodgetts and J Devey added a third point, and Hodgetts the fourth. After some even play in midfield the Heanor forwards ran through, and Shepherd scored. Heanor, however, could not keep up the pressure, the Villa once more making a strong attack on the visitor's goal, but Heanor played a plucky game up to the finish. They were, however, clearly overmatched, and the game ended: -

ASTON VILLA ……..4   HEANOR ……..……..1

PLAYERS:-

ASTON VILLA – Warner (goal), Evans, Coulton (backs),
H Devey, Cowan, Baird (half backs), Athersmith, Hare,
Devey, Hodgetts, and L Campbell (forwards).
HEANOR – J Carlin, (goal), R Wright, E Cotton (backs), J Timson,
J Peace, H Webb (half backs), R Jardine, J Stott (left wing), A
Carter, A Atkins (right wing), and W Sheppherd (centre).
LINESMEN – Messers A G Hines and M Churchill.
REFEREE – Mr Gough.

NOTTINGHAM EVENING POST MONDAY JANUARY 18TH 1892

The Villa were supposed to have the easiest task of the 32 clubs, but they found that the Heanor men were not to be despised, and up to half time had failed to score a goal. Once they broke through in the second portion they soon got four goals, and then to the unbounded joy of about 400 ardent Heanor supporters who had followed the team by the two special trains run by the Midland and Great Northern lines, the Midland Alliance men scored a goal. The Heanor players are worthy of every praise for the gallant fight they made, and the result is bound to do them a lot of good.

FURTHER INFORMATION

Heanor Town's 1891/92 FA Cup run.

First Qualifying round   Greenhalgh's 0 - 2 Heanor Town
At Field Mill, Mansfield

Second Qualifying round   Heanor Town 2 - 1 Staveley

Third Qualifying round   Newark 0 - 0 Heanor Town

Extra time agreed, Darkness stopped game

Replay   Heanor Town 6 - 1 Newark

Fourth Qualifying round   Mansfield 2 - 4 Heanor Town

First round (last 32)   Aston Villa 4 - 1 Heanor Town

Aston Villa's cup run continued until they eventually lost to West Bromich Albion 3 - 0 in the final.

Sources: Mansfield Reporter 9th October 1891, Ripley and Heanor News 30th October 1891, The Athletic News 16th November, 7th December 1891, The Football News 28th November 1891, The National Football museum.

Heanor Town FC 1891/92
Back row: H Freeman, R Cotton, R Wright, J Carlin, A Atkins, and Mr Hill.
Middle row: H Webb, J Timson, R Jardine, J Peace, and A Carter.
Front row: W Sheppard, and J Stott.
(© Picture The Past)

1893 MINERS STRIKE

EXTRAORDINARY SCENES AT ILKESTON

THE DERBYSHIRE COURIER
SATURDAY SEPTEMBER 9TH 1893

On Friday afternoon, when it became known at Ilkeston that some colliers had gone back to work at West Hallam Colliery, near that place, an immense crowd of men and women set off for that place to fetch the men out of the mine and escort them home with a public demonstration. Shortly after two o'clock some 2000 persons had invaded the colliery premises, clamouring for the men to be fetched out of the mine. Inspector Savory, of the Ilkeston police force, and two or three constables were quickly on the spot, and when the two men were got out of the pit a great procession was formed, and marched right through the main streets of Ilkeston, creating excitement. The two offenders were made to carry a banner, on which were depicted two black miners, with the legend "Blacklegs" painted across the banner, whilst from each end of the cross pole was suspended a black stocking. Inspector Savory marched immediately behind the two men, and was surrounded by a bodyguard of stalwart fellows. Immediately in front of the banner was a scratch band, consisting of concertinas, tin whistles, big drum &c., the instrumentalists making what din they could with their chosen martial instruments. Hooting for blacklegs was interspersed with cheers as the crowd passed the residences of well-known givers to the relief fund. The procession marched the men right to their homes in Cotmanhay, where the unlucky wights were only too glad to take refuge from the hooting crowd. Inspector Savory, mounting a chair, was promptly accorded silence. He urged the crowd to go quietly home and do no violence. He congratulated them upon the orderly manner in which they conducted themselves throughout the journey from the pit at West Hallam to the men's homes at Cotmanhay. Cheers were given to the Inspector, who acted with great tact, and so ended one of the most extraordinary scenes ever seen at Ilkeston.

DISTURBANCES IN DERBYSHIRE

THE NEWCASTLE DAILY CHRONICLE
TUESDAY OCTOBER 31ST 1893

POLICE CHARGES ON THE CROWD

A Telegram from Alfreton last night stated that at Ripley, Derbyshire, considerable excitement and disorder were created yesterday through the hostility of the miners who are idle against the action of some of their fellows in decending the Ripley Pit, belonging to the Butterley Company, in order to get coal to supply the colliery engines. Several men yesterday accepted the invitation of the company, and descended the pit. During the day, large crowds began to assemble in the vicinity of the colliery, and they become hostile and menacing that the 17th Lancers were sent for from Alfreton as well as a strong body of police. The colliery premises were guarded by constables, while the soldiers paraded in a field close by. When the men were turned out of the pit great excitement prevailed, and after clearing the approaches to the colliery, the police escorted them to their houses, followed by an exasperated crowd. Near the houses of some of the men in Havelock Street stones were thrown at the constables, and several of them were struck. The consequence was that the constables charged the crowd, using their truncheons freely, and several persons were more or less injured. Last night it was necessary to guard the homes of those who had descended the pit.

Havelock Street, Ripley in 2023.
Location of the miners strike disturbances in 1893.
(Author's collection)

MANCHESTER CITY V HEANOR TOWN

THE NOTTINGHAM EVENING POST
SATURDAY NOVEMBER 17TH 1894

A Friendly match between these teams was played at Manchester. here was a fair company of spectators. The City started, and by good passing immediately pressed, but Hopkins cleared from Sharples. Finnerhan then ran the ball down the field, but shot over the bar. Heanor next attacked, Williams saving splendidly. After this City pressed, Finnerhan scoring the first goal with a splendid shot, while when Heanor attacked the ball was shot over. Finnerhan again ran down the field, beating Carlin a second time. Hands for the City was well saved by Carlin. Heanor forced a corner, which was easily cleared, and the City again attacked. Offside against Meredith enabled Heanor to force them back, Butterworth scoring a goal for the visitors. From the kick off Meredith scored the third goal for City and from a corner Milarvie Headed over. Half time: - City three goals; Heanor one. The City attacked on resuming, Milarvie when in good position shooting over the bar. Sharples scored a fourth for the City after Carlin had cleared repeatedly, Heanor only occasionally crossing the halfway line. Widdowson, however, scored for them with a fast shot from Hardy's centre. From the centre kick Sharples again beat Carlin, Finnerhan scoring a sixth for the City, who added two more points afterwards. Result: - Manchester City eight goals; Heanor two.

Manchester City: - Wlliams (goal), Walker, Dyer (backs),
Smith, Jones, Nash (half backs), Meredith, Finnerhan,
Rowan, Sharples, and Milarvie (forwards)
Heanor: - R Carlin (goal), W Hopkins, S Carlin (backs), H
Webb, G Rose, J Connor (half backs), A Hardy, S Widdowson,
A Lees, G Allen, and C Butterworth (forwards)

Heanor Town F C 1893/94 - The season before Heanor Town played a friendly against Manchester City. Players R Carlin, S Carlin, H Webb, A Hardy and S Widdowson appear in this photo and within the 11 names on the team sheet Vs Manchester City.

Back: A Whitelaw, R Carlin, and S Carlin.

Middle: W Tailor, T Shrewsbury, J Peace, H Webb, and A Hardy.

Front: S Widdowson, T Rose and R Jardine.

(© Picture The Past)

FURTHER INFORMATION

1894 was the first year Manchester City played under the name of Manchester City. Previously to this the club had been known as Ardwick A F C. Heanor Town played City within the first 3 months of their first season known as Manchester City Football Club.

Sources: www.mancity.com

WIFE KILLED IN BED

THE MORNING LEADER LONDON
FRIDAY FEBRUARY 28TH 1896

A CRIME WHICH THE AUTHOR ATTRIBUTED TO
BEASTLY DRUNKNESS

At the Derbyshire Assizes yesterday, before Mr Justice Hawkins, a shoemaker named Samuel Rigby, aged 79, was charged with the wilful murder of his wife, aged 75, at South Normanton. The evidence was to effect that the prisoner, who lived on amicable terms with his wife, attacked her during the night, it is supposed with a poker, causing her injuries from which she died. The prisoner in pleading said "I cannot recollect , I was beastly drunk." According to the medical evidence the body of the deceased was covered with bruises, and she, in her depositions, said her husband had committed an unprovoked assault upon her. The prisoner was found guilty of manslaughter and he was sentenced to penal servitude for life, the judge remarking, that there was no doubt he had done his wife to death by savage cruelty.

TRAGEDY PREVENTED AT ALFRETON

THE DERBY MERCURY
WEDNESDAY APRIL 21ST 1897

A strange affair took place at Alfreton last week. As some miners were crossing the fields from Alfreton to Blackwell they noticed a young woman in the Alfreton brook. She had a child under her arms, under circumstances which seemed to suggest that it was her intention to drown the child and possibly herself as well. The woman was fetched out of the water, and she proved to be Harriett Mills, of Alma Street , Alfreton. The child a little girl of about eight months old, is illegitimate, and had evidently been in the water. The mother and child were brought home, and Dr Leary was called in; he applied a remedy of artificial respiration, and eventually the child was brought round. When found the mother said, "Let me alone,

I want to drowned myself." Afterwards the woman was arrested. At the Alfreton Police Court on Tuesday, before J Roberts Esq., Harriett Mills was charged with having attempted to murder her illegitimate child, Edith Ann Mills, eight month old, at Alfreton, on 12th April. – Thomas Cooper, coal miner, High Street , Swanwick, deposed that on Monday afternoon he was walking with George Clay along the footpath leading from Blackwell to Alfreton, when they saw a woman in the water. She was in a stooping position with a child in her arms. Witness could not see at first whether the child was in the water or not. When the woman heard them she raised herself up from the water with the child in her arms. They went across the water to her. She was standing up to her thighs in the water. The baby was dripping with wet, and was gasping for breath. Its lips and face was quite purple. Prisoner began screaming, and Clay said "What have you done it for?" She replied that she had not a friend in the world, and that all her brothers had turned against her. She also said (referring to the child), "oh, my little angel." She repeated that several times. Witness jumped into the water, took the baby from her, and pushed her towards the bank. Then Clay took hold of her hand and pulled her out. When they got her out of the water she began to be restless, and wanted to get into the water herself, saying "I will finish myself." In reply to Mr Walters as to what state the baby was in, he said he thought all the way that it would die. He turned it upside down for the water to run out of its mouth, and it began to revive. – Prisoner, who seemed much distressed, was remanded for eight days.

FURTHER INFORMATION

Harriett Mills was tried on the 12th July 1897 at the Derbyshire Summer Assizes and sentenced to imprisonment for 3 calendar months. During the trial Harriet Mills employer, Mrs Ann Mycroft said of Harriett that she had been in her service three years, and was quite willing to take her back. In passing sentence the Judge said he should not sentence the prisoner to undergo hard labour. She must go to gaol for three months without hard labour, and hoped that at the end of that time her mental condition would be fully restored.

Sources: England and Wales Crime, Prison and Punishment, 1770 – 1935.
The Derbyshire Courier Saturday 17th July 1897.

CELEBRATIONS OF THE QUEEN'S DIAMOND JUBILEE

THE RIPLEY AND HEANOR NEWS
FRIDAY JUNE 25TH 1897

RIPLEY

The celebrations of the Queen's Diamond Jubilee opened in a very pleasing and appropriate manner on Sunday morning, by the merry peals rung on the bells of the All Saints Church, where services of thanks giving were held morning and evening, for the blessings enjoyed throughout the British empire during the long reign of 60 years of Her Most Gracious Majesty, Queen Victoria. The preacher, morning and evening was the Vicar (Rev W E Bradstock) who alluded in fitting terms to the exemplary life which the Queen has led, and to the great changes which had taken place, especially in the mining industries of Ripley and the surrounding neighbourhood, since she ascended the throne. Special musical arrangements had been made, and each of the services concluded by singing the National Anthem. Similar services were conducted at St Johns Church, Green Hillocks, while at other places of worship in the town, special reference was made by the preachers to the long and prosperous reign of Her Majesty, the musical arrangements of the services having been made appropriately. All the services were well attended. In the afternoon at three o'clock a United Sunday School Demonstration was held. When the various Sunday Schools headed by their banners walked in procession to the Market Place, where they were arranged in order in front of a platform erected for the representatives. The Ripley United band was present, and several special hymns were heartily sung by the children, Mr J Caulton acting as conductor. Mr A Day presided, and the Rev C R Round delivered a stiring address, appropriate to the occaision, which was listened to very attentively by all present. There were also on the platform the Vicar (Rev W E Bradstock), the Rev S S Allsop, the Rev Giffard Dorey, and ministers of other denominations, along with various

Sunday School representatives. The proceedings throughout were of a very imposing character, terminated by the pronunciation of the Benediction. The Ripley Church Lads' Brigade was present under the command of Sergeant Instructor Pickering, and their order of marching and general conduct throughout was well worthy of mention as being of the best possible kind. The lads presented a smart appearance, which reflects the greatest credit on those responsible for their turnout. Flags were floating from the tower of All Saints' and other places during the day. On Tuesday the rejoicing caused an early stir amongst the inhabitants of the town, who were busily engaged in work of decoration. The general appearance of the various business premises was very gay, the display of bunting being on an elaborate scale, and carried out with exceptionally good taste. In addition to the numerous flags which were seen floating from the principal business firms and dwellings of the town, garlands, streamers, and evergreens might have been seen suspended across the streets at various points, bearing suitable mottoes, while some had nicely draped materials bearing the colours of red, white, and blue stretched across the front of their premises. Church Street, Oxford street, and the Market place were bedecked with bunting of almost every conceivable kind, as were Nottingham road, Chapel street, and Butterley hill. Several of the business firms were illuminated at night, and, in all, the scene was one to be remembered in the history of the town. At three o'clock in the afternoon the Butterley Detachment Sherwood Foresters (Derbyshire Regiment) marched from their headquarters, headed by the Volunteer Band, to the Market place. Here, under the direction of Sergeant Instructor Behenna, they were put through a course of manoeuvres, which was skilfully executed, after which the band played the National Anthem. Each man was then presented with a shilling. The Church Lads' Brigade was also present, and the scene on the Market place in all proved a very attractive feature of the day's programme. A good number of people assembled to witness this spectacle, and it proved very successful. At four o'clock, a free tea was provided for the scholars of the town at their respective schools, and those not attending any school were provided with tea at St John's School, as previously arranged by the committee. Mugs and medals are also provided, the mugs for children between the ages of 3 and 12 and those over that age medals. The mugs are being supplied by Messers Bourne and Son, of Denby Pottery, and the medals by Messers Ryland and Son, of Birmingham. After tea, the children were divided into two sections, one of which were drafted into a field on the Derby road, the other going to the field adjoining the Butterley Hall, where all kinds of games were freely indulged in. They were also provided with nuts, oranges and sweets. The Volunteer Band remained on the Market place, playing selections of music at intervals, until about half past five o'clock. Apart from the scholars treat, a meat tea was provided in the Public Hall, which was given by Mrs Crossley, sen, and Mr Jas Crossley, for old people over 60 years of age. The tea was served by Mrs Smith, confectioner, Market place. Something like 150 persons were present, who heartily appreciated the kindness which had been shown to them. The following rendered valuable assistance : - Mrs Lowthian, Miss Crossley, Mrs Capon, Mrs Clark, Miss Clark, Mrs Taylor, Mrs Douge, Mrs Wood, Mr W H Lowthian, Mr G M Capon, Rev T Scrimshaw, Mr H Clark, and others. The Rev T Scrimshaw presided. At the conclusion Mr W Walters moved a vote of thanks to Mrs Crossley and Mr Jas Crossley, and to all who rendered assistance, Mr Jas Crossley briefly responded and in doing so expressed the great pleasure it had given his mother and himself to provide the tea for them, and expressed hope that they had all enjoyed themselves. He also commented at some length upon the long reign of Her Majesty the Queen, referring to her noble attributes. He also spoke in high terms of the service rendered by Mr G M Capon, who had worked very hard indeed. The proceedings terminated by singing "God save the Queen." About ten o'clock a large concourse of people gathered around the bonfire, which was in a field on the Heage road, and which was lighted by Mrs Rouse and Mr R Argile. Previous to lighting the beacon, which was one of the best in the Midlands, rockets were fired at intervals. Mr G M Capon acted as secretary for the Jubilee Committee, and great praise is due to him for the manner in which he carried out his onerous duties.

CODNOR

Very few villages could boast of a much better celebration of the Diamond Jubilee of Her Majesty the Queen than that of Codnor. From the very commencement the inhabitants showed a disposition to make the festivities such as would never be forgotten by those who took part in them. A very representative committee was appointed to make the arrangements, and the united efforts on the part of those responsible culminated in a very enthusiastic gathering. What is most worthy of note in connection with the arrangements of the Codnor festivities was the mutual and united manner in which the members of the various religious denominations worked together. No prejudice arose to mar the proceedings, which were of a most lively and animated character. From one end of Codnor to the other was displayed such a variety of bunting and other kind of decorations, that no doubt could be left in the minds of anyone as to the respect and esteem in which Her Majesty the Queen was held. Jessop street, especially, presented a very pleasing aspect, numerous garlands stretched across the street, which for brightness of colour could scarcely have been surpassed, and in addition to these, flags were very much in evidence, which in all made up a very gay scene. Mill lane and Wright street had not been neglected in the matter of decoration, while the main road leading to Codnor Church was also nicely treated, as was Waingroves. In the morning at ten o'clock, a procession was formed in Codnor Market place, the order of which was as follows : - Members of the Parish Council, members of the committees, friendly societies, united choir, and the general public. The procession was headed by the Codnor U M F C Band, and paraded the village to the Parish Church, where a united thanksgiving service was held. The sacred edifice was crowded, the service being of a very hearty character, and will long be remembered by those who were present. The service opened with a hearty rendering of the National Anthem, after which the prayers were read by the Rev I P Peile and the lessons by the Rev J Spivey. The musical portion of the service was splendid rendered by the united choirs, of which there were six. Especially well treated were the Te Deum (Vaughan in D) and the anthem , "Happy are the people." The hymn, "O God help in ages past," was heartily sung by the congregation, after which the Vicar (Rev W Bates) preached an able sermon from the words of the 29th and 30th verses of the last chapter of Proverbs. The Vicar, in the course of his remarks, said they were met together to take part in a national thanks giving service to offer their thanks to Almighty God for sparing the life of Her Majesty the Queen to reign over her people with majestic grace and love for 60 years, and perhaps it would only be natural if he said, as an acknowledgement for their presence on that occasion, that he gave them a hearty welcome. They could join with one voice and one heart in returning thanks to Almighty God for the preservation of the Queen, who lived an exemplary life, and one which they might follow, and follow to the highest degree without the fear of danger. The rev gentleman spoke at some length on the good qualities of the Queen, and said it was not the fact that the Queen had reigned for a period of 60 years, which had called them together; it was not that which was in their minds; it was the noble exemplary life which she had led, and the glorious deeds done during her reign, which would be written with a pen of gold in some future days. It was these which they were proud Englishmen. They had had much to rejoice over during the Queen's reign. A great change had come over the nation, and there was a good deal following. He referred in high terms to the loyalty of our colonial friends, and asked how it was that Englishmen, as a nation were able to control so very many millions of people. How was it they had the power. He maintained that it was because English rule was the wisest and the best. Englishmen ought to feel proud of their country, and of the people, and offer up their thanks to Almighty God for the great blessings they had had during this long reign. The sermon was a very eloquent one and was listened to with rapt attention by all present. At 1.15 a public meeting was held, the Rev W Bates presiding. The meeting was addressed by Messers F C Corfield J P, W Hardy CC, and W Eyre. At the conclusion of the meeting the procession was reformed, and proceeded by the way of Mill lane, Wright street, and Jessop street, to the cemetery, when the unveiling of the commemoration tablet at the foot of the Jubilee Oak (1887) took place.

The people of Loscoe joined in the demonstration. After a few introductory remarks by Mr A F Pine, Mrs F C Corfield performed the ceremony. She said: Ladies and gentlemen and Mr Pine, - I thank you and the committee very much for asking me to unveil this tablet; it was very kind you to wish me to do so. As Mr Pine had already said we are commemorating two events, the planting of the Oak tree ten years ago at the time of the Queen's Jubilee, and today the 60th year of her glorious reign. It has been subscribed to by many loyal subjects in Codnor, Loscoe, and Waingroves, and I hope that both the tablet and oak will be looked at and venerated by many future generations. I dare say that many of us would like to have been in London today and seen the Queen, but as we cannot all be there we must do our best to make this a very happy day here, particularly to the children, so that the memory of this day and of our great and good Queen, who has done so much for us all, may live amongst us for a great many years. I now unveil this tablet. – Mr H Watson (Loscoe), in a few well-chosen sentences, proposed that a hearty vote of thanks be tendered Mrs Corfield for kindly consenting to unveil the tablet. – Mr Farnsworth said he believed the Diamond Jubilee celebration was one of the greatest events of the century, and certainly that was one of the best days he had seen in Codnor. It was pleasant to think of the millions of loyal hearts who were that day returning thanks to God for Victoria's long reign. All kinds and conditions of men, from palace to the workhouse were rejoicing on that auspicious day. When he was at Basford the other day, he saw the Union Jack floating from the highest tower they had. He rejoiced to think that the poor in the workhouse were not forgotten on that day, and that something was being done for them to make their lives brighter. (Hear, Hear.) He thought that Codnor had done well and shown their loyalty thoroughly. They certainly might have done something greater, but they would compare very favourably with their neighbours. (Hear, hear.) He was proud to think they had with them Mrs Corfield to perform the ceremony of unveiling that tablet, and he had very great pleasure in seconding the vote which had been proposed. Mrs Corfield came amongst them as one of themselves and he did not think a more popular lady could have been selected to perform the ceremony. Her kindness was indeed proverbial. (Applause.) – The motion was carried with acclamation. – Mr Corfield thanked them very much for the kind words which had been spoken respecting Mrs Corfield. He contended they were all one that day in doing honour to Her Majesty. There was one word mentioned to the effect that Mrs Corfield was one of themselves. He might state that she always came amongst them as one of them. They were all living together, she belonged to Codnor, and was always pleased to do anything she could for them. He was much obliged to them for the vote of thanks they had passed in her behalf. (Applause.) During this ceremony the scholars remained in rank on the road, and the procession afterwards returned through Waingroves. The procession was made a lively one, as in addition to the banners of the various Sunday Schools very many of the scholars carried flags, while a maypole representation looked exceedingly pretty. At 4 o'clock tea was provided in a field, attention being first devoted to the juniors. Old English sports were freely indulged in during the evening, which caused great amusement, and at dusk a grand display of fireworks took place. A huge mass of timber had been constructed in a pile reaching to a height of 48 feet, being 73 feet round the base, the timber being given by the Butterley Company. This was situated on High Holborn hill. A signal rocket was fired at 9.55, and the fire was lighted at 10 o'clock by Mr F C Corfield, there being at the time a very large concourse of people present. Over £42 was collected for the Codnor festivities, and the proceedings passed off very satisfactorily. Mr A F Pine officiated as secretary, and great praise is due to him and all those who in any way assisted in the work, as the arrangements were carried out splendidly.

The tablet revealed by Mrs F C Corfield in 1897 to commemorate Queen Victoria's diamond jubilee in St James Church, Codnor photographed in 2023.
(Author's collection)

RIPLEY AND HEANOR MEN AT THE BOER WAR

RIPLEY AND HEANOR NEWS
FRIDAY DECEMBER 29TH 1899

Letters from friends at the seat of war, however brief such may be, are always full of interest, and our Ripley readers in particular will be keenly interested in the appended letter, received by Mr Walter Bradley, of Greenwich, Ripley, from his brother Alfred Bradley, a special reserve man of the 1st Royal Scots. It is, of course, several weeks since Private Bradley left Ripley, and his friends have naturally been anxious as to his location and doings. The epistle, which is characteristics of the blunt soldier, and another instance of the eagerness which all our gallant soldiers have shown to give the Boers battle, and evidently written under difficulties with a blue pencil on a single sheet of writing paper, reads as follows : - "Capetown, December 1st 1899. Dear Walter, - Just a few lines, hoping to find you all well, as it leaves me well after twenty six days of misery. We are going to the front, and sooner the better. I should like to get a shot or two at the Boers. By the time you get this letter we shall be at it, "George" and myself are in the same company, He stands behind me. We go by train from the Cape for three days, if the Boers do not stop us. I hope they start; we are ready for them………..From your loving brother. Good Bye. PS Going to East London" The George referred to is Private Hodgkinson also of Ripley.

THE RIPLEY AND HEANOR NEWS
FRIDAY JUNE 1ST 1900
HEANOR AMBULANCE MAN AT THE FRONT

Mr Charles Blakey, Loscoe Road, Heanor, has received two letters from his son, Private 746 W Blakey, No.23 Field Hospital St John Ambulance Brigade R A M C Field Forces, South Africa. Writing on April 22nd. Private Blakey says : - " We arrived at Edenberg by train on Friday morning 20th, camping by night. On Saturday we set off on a 16 miles march to Reddersberg. From here we proceed up country as far as we are wanted. We travel at night on account of the intense heat during the daytime. We have fared very well up to now, plenty to eat and drink all that day. We have two hospital companies and one bearer company on the march with us, five ox waggons carrying the luggage, 16 oxen being attached to each waggon. When we were coming up the country we passed through a storm of moths, and air being thick and black with them. We arrived in Reddersberg on Sunday night, 6:30, just as the church bells were ringing for service. We have had no orders yet whether we go up the country or not. We expect to proceed further to join the 8th Division, who are fighting 15 miles from here. It seems a little more like being home for us tonight, as we are occupying a house that has been left by one of the Free Staters, and it is fully furnished and very comfortable indeed. The same house was used as the headquarters of Commandant Botha while the Boers were fighting in this district. I have had no letters since leaving Cape Town. You will be surprised when I tell you a pound loaf of bread costs 1s, fresh butter 2s per lb and eggs five for 1s, but we can purchase a chicken for 1s."

A Second letter, dated April 30th, Thabanchu Camp, Free State, says : - "We have arrived here from Edenberg, a distance of 76 miles, and we marched nearly all the way, the baggage being conveyed in ox waggons. We camped out each night except one, which we spent in Reddersberg. Our rations have not been quite as good as on the Gaika, but we cannot expect to have quite as good as on the ship. I should have liked for you to see us on the march from Edenberg. Some of our men had a job to hold up just before we came to a camp on the way, at the foot of the Thabanchu Mountains. One of the West Kent Regiment officers was shooting a bullock for food, when the bullet passed straight through it and killed a man that was standing behind it. Yesterday (Sunday) we heard Boer guns about three or four miles away, one shell passing right over our heads, whistling like a rocket does. We have seven or eight men in our hospital who came in yesterday from an engagement with the Boers"

PRIVATE HODGKINSON OF RIPLEY AT WEPENER

Pvt J Hodgkinson, of the Royal Scots, Mounted Infantry, has written to his father at Ripley from Bloemfontein, the following letter which is dated May 3rd : - " I am in the best of health. I suppose you heard how we took Stormberg, and since then I have been all over the country getting on at one place at night and off at daybreak the next morning. I have just had enough of it. I have been with three columns and have now joined Lord Roberts at Bloemfontein. I was at the taking of Bethulie. We were in the trenches for 14 hours, and then rushed the bridge and followed the enemy up to Springfontein, but they slipped us there and we rested for four days. They sent us then – the mounted – to Smithfield where we stopped two days. There were only 80 of us, and about 8,000 Boers about three hours ride from us, but they moved off at night, and we left in the morning, following them right through the State to Wepener, where we met the colonial troops. We took up a position and the Boers surrounded us – 1400 to about 9000 of the enemy. Once they sent in a flag of truce for us to surrender to save further bloodshed, we said "No, fight to a finish." So they bid us good bye in the morning with a shell from a 40 pounder. We had to saddle up and gallop into position under fire and great loss. They kept us in trenches for 17 days. We never got out and were knee deep in water, and they made five night attacks, but we repulsed them. We could hear them shout in English to rush, and our captain gave the word to fix bayonets, so they did not come much further. They used the 'pom-pom' to us."

PRIVATE BRADLEY OF RIPLEY IN THE TRENCHES 19 DAYS

Mr W Bradley, of Greenwich, Ripley, has received the following letter from his brother Pvt Alf Bradley, of the Royal Scots Mounted infantry dated May 5th, from Bloemfontein : - "Since I wrote to you last I have gone through a lot of fighting, and a good deal of hardship. After leaving Bethulie Bridge we went to Springfontein, and stopped there two days. From there we went to Wepener, a forced march of 100 miles, which took us three days. We stayed in Wepener three days and then went to Jammerburg Drift, about three miles outside Wepener. We were surrounded by 10,000 Boers, our forces all told being 1400 and seven guns. The Boers started to shell us on April 9th, and made an attack the same day. The Royal Scots Mounted lost three killed and seven wounded. We were in trenches for 19 days and could not leave them, and for five days and nights it poured down with rain, but we got relieved at last. Our casualties were Royal Scots, three killed, 12 seriously wounded and many slightly; Cape Mounted Police, 20 killed and 90 wounded; Brabant's Horse, 70 killed and wounded. We lost over 500 horses – the Royal Scots, 48. We have just landed at Bloemfontein, and are getting a bit of rest and rig out of clothing, which we all need, and then we are going to join Roberts' forces. I hope you got the Queen's chocolate box. I sent it from Springfontein on the 19th of March. I have not got the box you spoke of in your letter, but as soon as I do I will send you word. I have got some curios, but cannot send them very well. I shall try and bring some back with me if I have the chance, but it is impossible to keep anything long with moving so often. Did you see an account of our fight at Jammerberg Drift in the papers? It was there we lost the most; it was a hornet's nest, if you like. We were up to the waist in water many times during the heavy rain we got for five days."

A Chocolate box/tin like the one Private Alfred Bradley writes about sending home in his letter.

(Image courtesy of Vintage Frog)

A NATION'S LOSS

THE RIPLEY AND HEANOR NEWS
FRIDAY JANUARY 25TH 1901

DEATH OF QUEEN VICTORIA
AN EMPIRE GRIEVES

It was with the profound grief that the nation learnt of the death of Her Most Gracious Majesty Queen Victoria, which took on Tuesday evening at half past six at Osborne, in the presence of her children and grandchildren. The Queens illness was very brief. The first official allusion being made to it at the end of last week. Some months ago she began to suffer from sleeplessness, and naturally lost strength in consequence. Her regular habits were broken up, but although she retired earlier at night to rise later in the morning and forewent her drives, Her Majesty, although advised by her medical advisors, refused to discontinue the routine work which devolved upon her as head of the State. She continued to see Ministers and State officials, and as late as Tuesday, the 15th, had an interview at Osborne of considerable length with Lord Roberts. From thence however the Queen began to exhibit graver signs of prostration, and on Saturday a bulletin was issued describing the Queen as suffering from physical prostration accompanied by symptoms that caused anxiety. Gradually Her Majesty sank, and passed peacefully away in her sleep on Tuesday evening, after having recognised the several members of the Royal Family gathered round her bedside at noon. Queen Victoria's reign has been the longest in English history. It has lasted 63 years, seven months, and two days. And not only has she reigned over us the longest of any monarch, but she has lived the longest by four days. On Friday last she passed the age of George III. Born at Kensington Palace on 24th May 1819, Her Majesty was the only child of H.R.H Edward, Duke of Kent, fourth son of George III. When eighteen she succeeded her uncle, William IV. – June 20th , 1837, and was crowned on June 28th , 1838. She was married on February 10th , 1840, to her cousin, Prince Albert Augustus Charles Emanuel

, Duke of Saxony, and Prince of Saxe-Coburg-Gotha, but after twenty one years of married life Her Majesty was left a widow, Prince Consort dying on December 14th, 1861. There were nine children by the marriage, viz., Victoria Adelaide Mary Louisa, Empress Fredrick of Germany, mother of the present German Emperor; Albert Edward, Prince of Wales, born Nov 9th, 1841, and married March 10th 1863; Alice Maude Mary, born April 25th, 1843 married in 1862, died December 14th, 1878; Alfred Ernest Albert, Duke of Edinburgh, born August 6th, 1844, and married January 23rd, 1874; Helena Augusta Victoria, born May 25th, 1846, married July 5th, 1866; Louise Caroline Alberta, born March 18th, 1848, married March 21st, 1871, to the Marquis of lorne, K.T. ; Arthur William Patrick Albert, Duke of Connaught, born May 1st 1850, married March 13th, 1879 ; Leopold George Duncan Albert, Duke of Albany, born April 7th, 1853, married April 27th, 1882 ; and Beatrice Mary Victoria Fodora, born April 14th , 1857, married July 29th, 1885. Few people indeed realised how hard our Queen, most conscientious of monarchs, worked for the good of the realm. The welfare of her people was ever in her mind since that memorable early morning, when the beautiful young Princess of eighteen, called from her bed to hear from the lips of Prelate and Statesman that the King was dead and she was Queen, registered a mental vow ever to discharge to the best of her capacity the immense respon-sibilities of Empire laid upon her. "I will be good," has been the Princess Victoria's brave resolve, when in girlhood the Queenly responsibilities of her future were first unfolded to her young mind. During the eighty two years she lived, and particularly during the sixty four years she reigned, Victoria the great and the good afforded the brightest example of womanly nobility and queenly virtue. We look back with reverential admiration on her twenty one years of the brightest, sweetest maidenhood; on her twenty one years of gracious wifehood – an unbroken sacrament of the purest joys of domestic love; and on her forty years of unselfish, dignified widowhood, consecrated to an undying affection, which was only shared in her heart with her unceasing care for her subjects. Some hearts are seared and closed by grief. The Queen's noble heart, wounded by the greatest sorrow that ever happened to a woman only opened wider, in sympathy with the sorrows of all around. Was there war, famine, pestilence, disaster, or private sorrow, coming under the Queen's notice, her affectionate solicitude was always manifest, and her gracious, kindly, tactful, thoughtful messages of sympathy went direct from heart to heart. Of the Divine mystery of suffering the Queen had full share. To crown her sorrows in the last year of her reign she suffered keenly with the suffering of her brave troops in South Africa, and sympathised sorrowfully in the bereavements that many who sent husbands and sons to the front have sustained. But neither the burden of private grief or public sorrows diverted Her Majesty's mind from public affairs. She worked on steadily for the good of her vast and growing Empire. None but those privileged to enjoy her sage counsel can realise the thought and skill she brought to bear on the duties of a sovereign. None but those who are in deepest secrets of diplomacy know how powerful was the Queen's influence in checking forward ambition and preserving the peace of the world. But all of us can realise what a vast gift to civilization has been her long reign. Lovely in life, beautiful in her virtues, she has saved monarchy. Not so much in this country, where the perfection of constitutional union between Throne and State has been reached, but in the wide world, Republic-anism has waned, and Socialism is withering in the fierce pure light that beats upon the throne of England. With such a Sovereign to reign, monarchy is a perfect institution; and we wonder not that the world, which a generation ago was disposed to run amuck at all thrones, looking at the lofty picture of perfect monarchism in England, has inclined back to the old belief that after all a crowned head is the best head of the state. She ruled with a power which would have been amazing had we not understood its secret, which was that in all she undertook she was sincere. Her memory can never die. The traditions she leaves behind her will beautify our history to the end of time. In this thought, and the knowledge that the whole of the civilised world shares our profound sorrow, we find consolation in this dark hour.